W9-AHD-494

THE BIG DATA-DRIVEN BUSINESS

HOW TO USE BIG DATA TO WIN CUSTOMERS, BEAT COMPETITORS, AND BOOST PROFITS

RUSSELL GLASS · SEAN CALLAHAN

WILEY

Cover design: Wiley

Copyright © 2015 by LinkedIn Corp. All rights reserved.

Published by John Wiley & Sons, Inc., Hoboken, New Jersey.
Published simultaneously in Canada.

No part of this publication may be reproduced, stored in a retrieval system, or transmitted in any form or by any means, electronic, mechanical, photocopying, recording, scanning, or otherwise, except as permitted under Section 107 or 108 of the 1976 United States Copyright Act, without either the prior written permission of the Publisher, or authorization through payment of the appropriate per-copy fee to the Copyright Clearance Center, 222 Rosewood Drive, Danvers, MA 01923, (978) 750-8400, fax (978) 646-8600, or on the web at www.copyright.com. Requests to the Publisher for permission should be addressed to the Permissions Department, John Wiley & Sons, Inc., 111 River Street, Hoboken, NJ 07030, (201) 748-6011, fax (201) 748-6008, or online at www.wiley.com/go/permissions.

Limit of Liability/Disclaimer of Warranty: While the publisher and authors have used their best efforts in preparing this book, they make no representations or warranties with respect to the accuracy or completeness of the contents of this book and specifically disclaim any implied warranties of merchantability or fitness for a particular purpose. No warranty may be created or extended by sales representatives or written sales materials. The advice and strategies contained herein may not be suitable for your situation. You should consult with a professional where appropriate. Neither the publisher nor the authors shall be liable for damages arising herefrom.

For general information about our other products and services, please contact our Customer Care Department within the United States at (800) 762-2974, outside the United States at (317) 572-3993 or fax (317) 572-4002.

Wiley publishes in a variety of print and electronic formats and by print-on-demand. Some material included with standard print versions of this book may not be included in e-books or in print-on-demand. If this book refers to media such as a CD or DVD that is not included in the version you purchased, you may download this material at http://booksupport.wiley.com. For more information about Wiley products, visit www.wiley.com.

ISBN 9781118889800 (cloth); ISBN 9781118889787 (ebk); ISBN 9781118889848 (ebk)

Printed in the United States of America

10 9 8 7 6 5 4 3 2 1

Contents

Acknowledgments

Russ would like to thank his wife, Robin, and his three lovely girls—Ava, Mackenzie, and Annika—for having the patience to put up with him every day.

Sean would like to thank his wife, Nancy, and his daughters—Sophie and Charlotte—for understanding the occasional weekends and late nights that were devoted to writing this book. He would also like to thank his mom and dad for reading to him as a boy and giving him a lifelong love of stories.

Together, Russ and Sean want to thank all of the Bizonians and our new colleagues at LinkedIn who helped with the creation of this book.

They also thank all of the people who shared their insights with them and who were indispensable in shaping the ideas contained in this book.

Introduction: Why We Wrote This Book, and How It Can Help You

We decided to write a book about big data and its impact on businesses, after many years working in and around companies and with executives who were seeing, increasingly, how data could change the courses of their careers and the trajectories of the businesses they worked for. We also saw incredible big data stories starting to hit the public's consciousness. There was *Moneyball* (W.W. Norton, 2003), the book by Michael Lewis about how Oakland Athletics general manager Billy Beane gained a huge advantage through big data. More recently, there was *The Signal and the Noise* (Penguin, 2012), Nate Silver's book exploring why so many predictions fail because of a lack of big data—or because of a misinterpretation of it.

Despite its obvious power, the understanding and use of big data have remained surprisingly sporadic in the business world. We see three types of people:

1. The Pioneers, who are embracing the troves of data that they have access to and who are truly transforming the way businesses are run and how customer communication is done.

2. The Frozen, who either don't know how to get started or don't seem to want to uncover the truths that data might deliver.
3. The Denialists, who don't believe that big data has any value to deliver and whose businesses are dead or dying.

The first group is far outnumbered by the latter two.

We realized that those people who are stuck can learn a great deal from the Pioneers who have come before them. These Pioneers are not only breaking new ground but executing at a high level, and all the while they are solving technological, organizational, and cultural issues to capture and use data to deliver outsized returns on investment. These Pioneers are delivering great experiences for their prospects and clients. They are giving rise to greater truth and better decisions by making more data available in boardrooms. And they are helping to create companies that truly understand what their customer needs are now and will be in the future.

The people and stories we highlight in this book are designed to bring you insight into the first waves of a sea change in how business is and will be done. Not only have they already brought huge upside into their organizations, but they are also positioning their companies to be long-term leaders in a highly competitive world.

We hope you find the journey as interesting as we do and come away with some insights on why and how big data is changing and should change the way business functions—whether within tiny start-ups or within the largest enterprises in the world. Our thesis starts with a simple premise: *the companies that most effectively use big data to gain insight into their customers and act on that data will win*. Be data-driven and customer focused, and you will reap the benefits.

We aim to show you how it's being done, and how you can get started. But first, let's go back to when the earth was still thought to be flat.

CHAPTER 1

Big Data, Big Benefits

Data, information, facts—whatever term you want to use, collecting and analyzing data have played a crucial part in humankind's ability to survive and to thrive since the dawn of consciousness. The earliest humans shared with each other what they knew of the world from their brains, those powerful catalogers of data in their skulls: hunt now, not later; eat this, not that; sleep here, not there.

Data is how we understand our world, and data has the capability to take us far beyond the surface impressions that our senses give us. Even though the world may appear flat to the eye, the ancient Greeks determined that the earth was round. In 240 BC, Eratosthenes used the different angles of shadows in two locations at high noon on the summer solstice to calculate the planet's circumference with remarkable accuracy—to within 1.6 percent.

Much of the mathematics, geometry, and other information compiled and shared by the likes of Eratosthenes essentially disappeared as the Dark Ages descended after the fall of Rome. But with Johannes Gutenberg's invention of the printing press in 1440—as statistician and writer Nate Silver points out in his book *The Signal and the Noise*—the amount of information available to societies again began to grow. Printed content enabled data to grow exponentially.

With his mind soaking up an expanding ocean of data created by these newly printed books, a sixteenth-century Roman Catholic church administrator named Nicolaus Copernicus wrote his own book, *De Revolutionibus Orbium Coelestium*, which used mathematical calculations and observations—data—to prove the idea that the earth revolved around the sun. This notion wasn't widely accepted in a time ruled by the Catholic Church, which was vigorously opposed to the idea that heaven was mutable and that the earth wasn't the center of it. Copernicus didn't allow his book to be published while he was alive, fearing a backlash from the Church he served. Despite the Church's longtime opposition, the data—and the truth—were eventually published.

The advent of computers has allowed data to grow at an even more mind-boggling rate. IBM's "Big Data at the Speed of Business" website says that we create 2.5 quintillion bytes of data every day, which means that 90 percent of the data in the world has been created in the past two years. The sheer amount of data and our growing ability to process it has led to the coining of the term *big data*.

The increasing ability of computers to process and store data was predicted by Gordon Moore, the cofounder of Intel, in the mid-1960s, and is at the heart of the rise of Silicon Valley as a global economic force. Moore formulated what is known as Moore's law, which holds that the number of transistors on a computer chip will double approximately every two years.

The result of this law's fulfillment is that the ability to process and store data becomes faster, easier, and cheaper. Progress, as evidenced by products such as smartphones and concepts such as cloud computing, happens quickly in the technology sector.

The fulfillment of Moore's law has created what's known as big data. In a narrow sense, big data is the incredibly fast analysis (enabled by increased processing speeds and cheaper storage) of massive sets of unstructured data to find previously unavailable insights. In a larger sense, big data is the lattice of computers, mobile phones, and other digital devices that create streams of data that organizations can analyze to gain actionable insights.

Another Moore, Geoffrey, has built his philosophy of marketing technology, which he outlines in books such as *Crossing the Chasm* (HarperBusiness, 1991) and *Inside the Tornado* (HarperBusiness, 1995), around Moore's law. "We have this incredible information processing engine that has just gotten more and more and more productive, so network, bandwidth, and storage keep having this exponential reduction in cost and expansion of scale," Geoffrey Moore said. "Pretty soon the next generation comes along, and they just design from a completely different set of assumptions."

In the past, paradigm shifts used to takes decades. "Now it feels like a single decade is kind of like the unit of a paradigm's life," Geoffrey Moore said.

The amazing rise of companies like Google shows the power of big data and its ability to transform not only the world of business, but the world as a whole. While big data has its skeptics, who say that big data is a fad that cannot possibly deliver on its overblown promise, the more likely reality is that the value of big data is, in fact, being underestimated. Big data—particularly for businesses and especially for marketing departments—is poised to have a profound and far-reaching impact on commerce and shareholder value. As it did for Eratosthenes, as it did for Copernicus, and as it may be doing for your company today, data will reveal the underlying truth of the world for those willing to work to see it.

Evidence that big data is much more than hype is undeniable. Big data has impacted everything from sports to politics. Case in point: even as Mitt Romney was climbing the national polls after triumphing in his first debate with President Obama during the 2012 election campaigns, Nate Silver predicted an Obama victory. Silver, a big data practitioner in baseball before he moved on to politics, stuck to his guns—and to his data. He relied on the data he blended from analyzing myriad polls. In the end, the Republicans used data to predict the result they wanted, while Silver looked more deeply into the data to predict the result that actually happened—down to the specific electoral vote count and a victory for Barack Obama.

While Nate Silver used data to accurately predict the election outcome, Dan Siroker, now the CEO of Optimizely, used data to make that outcome actually happen.

Siroker was a Google employee when he saw then-candidate Obama speak to executives at the company in 2007. Obama spoke about bringing Silicon Valley's digital and data expertise to government. Siroker was impressed. "I decided after the talk to fly to Chicago two weeks later, signed up as a volunteer, and eventually turned that into a job as the director of analytics for the Obama campaign," he said.

At Google, Siroker was an advocate of A/B testing—a process that pits different variables in landing pages, e-mail subject lines, or display ads against each other to determine which are the most effective. He brought this expertise to the Obama campaign. "I was tasked with figuring out how to use data to help make better decisions," Siroker said, "and it naturally led to website optimization and A/B testing."

He said the Obama campaign had to experiment by taking advantage of data and technology, because it had no choice. "They were third behind John Edwards and Hillary Clinton," he said. "They were forced to say, 'If we do the same thing every other campaign does, we'll end up like how everyone else thinks we're going to end up—which is third.' And so they said, 'Take risks.'"

In a blog post for Optimizely, Siroker explained how a series of A/B tests, which certainly don't seem so risky in retrospect, helped the 2008 Obama campaign raise an additional $60 million. On the campaign's website splash page, Siroker and his team tested six main visuals (three videos and three photographs) and four different calls to action (CTAs) ("join us now," "sign up now," "sign up," and "learn more"). The campaign tested a matrix of 24 combinations—all the potential permutations of images and CTAs.

Siroker wrote in the blog post that his team was convinced that a short inspirational video would win. The campaign tested each combination, judging them on the number of visitors who supplied e-mail addresses. The test analyzed the results of more than 300,000 visitors, which meant that each of the 24 permutations was viewed by about 12,500 people on average.

The results? The combination of the "learn more" CTA and a photo of the candidate with his wife and children posted the best performance. That combination resulted in 11.6 percent of visitors sharing their e-mail addresses compared with just 8.26 percent as the average. That meant the winning combination delivered a 40.6 percent improvement over the other combinations.

In the post, Siroker does the math. Because more than 10 million people ultimately saw the splash page, the winning combination delivered about 2.88 million more e-mail addresses. That led to 288,000 more volunteers, and—because each e-mail address averaged $21 in contributions—an additional $60 million for the campaign.

And what about the team's pretest favorite video? In his blog post, Siroker wrote, "Before we ran the experiment, the campaign staff heavily favored 'Sam's Video.' Had we not run this experiment, we would have very likely used that video on the splash page. That would have been a huge mistake since it turns out that all of the videos did worse than all of the images."

This experiment was just one of a myriad conducted in the Obama campaign's digital laboratory. "The Obama campaign is a great example of how they used data to win and the big influence that data had was on our ability to find campaign volunteers, do fund-raising, get out the vote, all of those things that were conversion events," Siroker said. ". . . We showed you can use data to help increase your conversion rate in an experiment, and that fundamentally was the key to the Obama campaign in 2008."

Siroker took the lessons learned from the Obama campaign and poured them into Optimizely, a company that helps marketers optimize websites and other digital marketing tactics. "Up until today, most marketers have spent a lot of time on acquisition—getting people to come to the website," he said. "Not everybody who shows up to your website turns into a customer, so it's about optimization. How do we get all those people—who we're spending a ton of money to get to show up—how do we turn them into customers?"

The arena where big data is having the largest impact today and where businesses may see the largest impact is the marketing department. In the past, long before companies like Optimizely, even great marketers—true believers like John Wanamaker—had a hard time proving that marketing worked. Wanamaker, a department store pioneer, reputedly said, "Half the money I spend on advertising is wasted; the trouble is I don't know which half."

Those words have lived on long after Wanamaker passed away in 1922. As a testament to how hard it has been to measure success in advertising, that remark has had a long shelf life. For decades, marketers used Wanamaker's words to shrug their shoulders as they justified spending on tactics they believed were working—even though they usually couldn't provide proof.

But the rise of big data is making that statement as dead as Mr. Wanamaker himself.

A recent television ad from software company Adobe promoting its Marketing Cloud shows how important data can be to the marketing team—and how damaging the wrong data can be to the entire company. The ad is a perfect representation of how the data-driven marketing department is at the center of the enterprise these days. The commercial, titled "Click, Baby, Click!," opens in the dark, dingy office of a fictional company, Encyclopedia Atlantica. Two guys wearing neckties report a surge in web activity. They inform the boss, "Clicks are off the charts!" He, in turn, calls an overseas supplier, telling him, "Yoshi. It's Walt. We're back!" Set to Edvard Grieg's short anthem "In the Hall of the Mountain King," the phone call sends printing presses into motion, causes tractor trailers and container ships to be loaded with Encyclopedia Atlanticas, forces more trees to be cut down, and leads to wood pulp futures taking a big jump.

Then comes the kicker. The ad closes by revealing the real reason that the Encyclopedia Atlantica website was seeing all those clicks: a toddler is playing with a tablet and pressing the "buy now" button on the encyclopedia website—over and over and over again.

Adobe finishes the ad by asking viewers: "Do you know what your marketing is doing? We can help." Aside from making a great case for the Adobe Marketing Cloud, this TV spot is a commentary on how the data rolling into the marketing department influences—for better or for worse—the rest of the enterprise. Executives make decisions based on this customer data, and these decisions determine how resources will be allocated throughout the company—and perhaps throughout an industry. With so much riding on the data, it had better be right.

In this digital age, leading marketers are embracing software platforms that deliver cascades of data. The software platforms that marketers are making use of include marketing automation systems, customer relationship management systems, data management platforms, and analytics tools to help make sense of what is happening. The most effective strategy is for companies to tie together the elements of this software, which together are known as the marketing stack. This allows the marketing team to see a complete picture—a 360-degree view—of how prospects and customers are behaving. With this insight about the target market, not only can the marketing team serve relevant messages to the right people at the right time, but it can also anticipate their needs and perhaps even create the products their customer base didn't even know it wanted.

Beyond the marketing department, data about the customer also flows into companies via e-commerce platforms, customer service call centers, and billing and payment records. The corporations that will benefit the most from their data are the ones that will bring all this information into a central repository. This centralized data repository should be managed by the marketing team, since they have more insight into the customers than another department would. How customers discover products or services, make purchasing decisions, and share their experiences—commonly referred to as the buyer journey—has changed dramatically. In the days before the Internet, potential clients researching products had little choice but to pick up a phone and call a sales representative to get more information about what they wanted to buy. Or, in the retail sector, they simply entered the store. In this new paradigm, it is not the sales department or the salesperson that is closest to the customer, as it was in the past.

Now it is the marketing department that has the clearest insight into the customer. In a 2012 blog post, Forrester Research analyst Lori Wizdo wrote that a potential customer can be 90 percent through the buyer journey before contacting a vendor. Prospects can research in solitude online via Google, by consulting LinkedIn groups, by browsing product reviews online, and by anonymously visiting vendor websites.

Through new software and platforms, marketing teams can see what Steve Woods, former Eloqua CTO and now the CTO of Nudge, calls the customer's "digital body language." By knowing what part of the website a prospect has visited, what e-mail newsletters she has signed up for, and what white papers she has downloaded, the marketing department understands where that prospect is in her buyer journey.

All of this points to the marketing department owning the customer life cycle and the customer relationship in the digital age. This fact will lead to the growing responsibility of the marketing department. Marketing has not always been thought of so highly. It has been derided as "the toy department," a part of the company that often had to beg the financial department for money to create branding ads. Using marketing automation tools, marketers are better able to identify which specific marketing tactics are generating return on investment.

Meagen Eisenberg, vice president of customer marketing at DocuSign, was recently asked if the Wanamaker remark about advertising and its effectiveness still had relevance. "I definitely think the quote is obsolete," Eisenberg said in a 2013 Digital Marketing Remix webinar. "When it comes to online marketing, I feel confident that the metrics, tracking, and technology we have today can prove what spend is working and what spend is not."

Marketing automation platforms such as Eloqua now enable marketers to quickly assess whether their branding and nurturing programs are driving conversions and generating revenue.

Use of a well-informed marketing stack is making the marketing department a more effective part of the business. Because of this increasing importance of software to the marketing department, Gartner analyst Laura McLellan projected in 2012 that the chief marketing officer (CMO) will spend more on information technology (IT) than the chief information officer (CIO) by 2017. Many CMOs, such as Motorola Solutions' Eduardo Conrado, already oversee both marketing and IT. This dual role of the marketing department reflects how central marketing data is becoming to the financial health of businesses.

Not only will the role of marketing become more critical for corporations, but former CMOs will be front and center in the next crop of great CEOs. This trend is already taking shape: Royal Dutch Shell, Audi, Mercedes-Benz, and others have all recently named CMOs as their chief executives. The movement of CMO to CEO is inevitable since other executives don't have the same amount of power to understand and solve customer problems, create brand loyalty, or move shareholder value today as quickly or as effectively as the CMO.

Marketing will no longer be defined by John Wanamaker's rather helpless-sounding quote. Instead, management guru Peter F. Drucker said words that we think are now more appropriate: "Business has only two functions: marketing and innovation."

We would add, ". . . and both of them will be led by the CMO."

In the marketing department and elsewhere, every corporation in the world is using big data to some degree. The winners will create cultures that embrace big data, employing data scientists to analyze data and draw conclusions that may contradict the company's assumptions, and to take action that takes advantage of the truth that the data reveals. The losers will use data to reinforce their own erroneous conclusions. This is not speculation. It is happening right now.

BlackBerry, which had what appeared to be an unassailable market share in smartphones, particularly among enterprise customers, initially shrugged off the launch of the Apple iPhone. But BlackBerry was ignoring the data. BlackBerry described the iPhone as a niche product aimed at consumers, but the revolutionary phone from Apple was making huge inroads not only with consumers but with BlackBerry's core business customers.

Nonetheless, BlackBerry thought its enterprise dominance made it safe. But by the time it became widely known that the iPhone, with its touch screen and excellent Internet access, was a serious competitor for business customers, BlackBerry was steamrolled by Apple's momentum, even losing its place in the enterprise to Apple and Google's Android. While many say the iPhone was a product created by Steve Jobs's magical intuition, Apple understood—from up-to-the-minute data being gathered by its proprietary retail stores and from its success with the iPod—that consumers would pay for a product that would combine their iPod with mobile phones and with the Internet access of their laptops.

In the end, both BlackBerry and Apple had access to data about the marketplace. One company, however, didn't have the culture to take advantage of the data. The other did, and it was the company that triumphed.

Of course, it's easy to say in retrospect that the data pointed to Apple's success and BlackBerry's demise. So we'll point to an industry that is ignoring the data that points to a systematic erosion in its business: the cable and satellite TV sector. Two "I Want Media" tweets, released seconds apart on Twitter, reveal the level of denial. The first tweet: "Report: Pay TV loses 113,000 Customers in Quarter." The second tweet: "Dish Says Too Early for Web to Challenge Pay TV."

Where are those customers going? They're going to YouTube, and they're going to Netflix, Hulu, Roku, and other alternatives. And if Dish and other pay TV companies are in denial and not addressing the problems the data is telling them quite directly, they are in for the same fate that befell BlackBerry.

The companies that create a culture that has intense focus on the customer through data, that values analyzing data, that is open to the truths data analysis reveals, and that has the guts to act on those conclusions will be the companies that prevail. The benefits of big data are available to any company, of any size, in any industry. Establishing a system that gathers and analyzes the data being generated by customers will deliver insights and reveal opportunities that you can't realize in any other way. History shows that competitive advantage and outsized shareholder value will follow.

CHAPTER 2

The Evolution of the Customer-Focused, Data-Driven Business

Having a strong focus on customers is nothing new. Neither is using data to better understand your customers. In fact, companies that have combined these approaches are among the standouts in business history.

In the late nineteenth century, two entrepreneurs, a thousand miles apart, established famed department stores built on a philosophy of serving the customer. In Chicago in 1862, Marshall Field founded the company that would become his eponymous department store. At Marshall Field's, the term *customer* and customizing the experience of each buyer were core to the business model. Field implemented two guiding principles at his store: "Give the lady what she wants" and "The customer is always right," according to Donald L. Miller's *City of the Century* (Simon & Schuster, 1996).

In those days when there were no databases or computers, it was difficult to measure exactly how well Field's stores lived up to those two principles with individual customers. But the old-fashioned ledger demonstrated the success of Marshall Field. By 1894, Field was successful enough to pledge $1 million (roughly $25 million in today's money) to the founding of the Field Museum of Natural History in Chicago.

Across the country in Philadelphia, John Wanamaker founded his own eponymous store in 1861. Like Field, the customer experience was central to the business model. Wanamaker eliminated haggling (he is said to have invented the price tag), and allowed returns—revolutionary concepts at the time. One of his stores was the first retail establishment to install electric lighting. By focusing on innovating with the customer in mind, Wanamaker saw his business flourish. In 1910, he built what has been described as a massive "palace" for his customers on a square block in Philadelphia's Center City, according to PBS's *They Made America*.

Those advances alone were enough to land Wanamaker a place among retailing's master innovators. But he also blazed trails in marketing. He invented the "white sale." His was the first department store to run half-page and full-page newspaper ads. Wanamaker's was also the first retailer to hire a full-time copywriter, John Emory Powers; during his tenure creating marketing copy for Wanamaker's, the company's revenues doubled from $4 million to $8 million.

In an era when hyperbole ruled advertising, Powers went against the grain and attempted to speak the plain truth in the advertisements he wrote for Wanamaker's. For instance, after he was told that the department store was trying to push "rotten gossamers," he wrote an ad that featured the line "We have a lot of rotten gossamers and things we want to get rid of." Legend has it that the gossamers were sold out by noon the day the ad ran.

With results like that, Wanamaker was a true believer in the value of advertising. But, like the marketing-oriented executives who followed him, he wanted more. He wanted data on how his advertisements were performing, which was in short supply in the print age and which is why Wanamaker reputedly said, "Half the money I spend on advertising is wasted; the trouble is I don't know which half."

While Wanamaker and Field established businesses that served the more cosmopolitan customers living in cities, in 1893 Richard Sears and Alvah Warren Roebuck established Sears, Roebuck & Company to serve customers in the farmlands. Through an unwanted delivery of a watch shipment in 1886, Sears gained an insight into a key data point: general stores serving rural areas were charging prices on goods that Sears could undercut by serving a broader market. By understanding both the marketplace and customer behavior, Sears built a mail order catalog business that Investopedia describes as the "Amazon.com of its day."

Here's the story: While Sears was working as a railroad agent in Minnesota, a shipment of wholesale watches arrived for the local jewelry store. When the store refused the delivery, Sears stepped in and bought the watches. He found that even though these watches typically retailed for $25 in stores, he could sell them for as little as $14 and still make a profit.

Sears moved to Chicago to take advantage of the city's position as a railroad hub and Sears, Roebuck & Company began its ascent by selling watches and jewelry via a mail order catalog, but rapidly increased the variety of products customers could buy and have delivered to their door.

Local store owners were not able to purchase the bulk quantities or offer the pricing or distribution that Sears, Roebuck could. Threatened by the new business, local shops intercepted and even burned the catalogs.

In the 1906 catalog, according to *Illinois History* magazine, Sears responded by providing its customers with some basic truth and data—some pretty devastating information that offered insight into the business practices of the general store merchants: "As a rule, the merchant from whom you buy adds little profit to the cost of goods as he can possibly afford to add. For example, a certain article in our catalog is quoted at $1.00, while your hardware merchant asks for $1.50 for that same article. . . ."

Eventually, the Sears catalog became a 500-page behemoth that expanded far beyond watches. The catalog even sold ready-to-assemble houses that were shipped via rail.

John Deere is another iconic corporation that caters to rural customers and thrives because of its focus on designing and delivering products its customers need—both through its products and through its content. Joe Pulizzi, founder of the Content Marketing Institute, recognizes John Deere as one of the first companies to use content marketing to build their customer base. That's because in 1895 Deere began publishing a magazine that was full of information to help customers (and prospects) become better farmers. The magazine, called *The Furrow*, is still published today.

While *The Furrow*'s foremost purpose is to deliver valuable content to its readership, it also fosters a sense of community, establishes brand recognition, and offers insight into the John Deere customer base. Subscribers to the magazine provide their names and mailing addresses as well as information about their businesses, which in turn provides John Deere with a database containing a wealth of knowledge about both customers and prospects. How many customers and prospects can John Deere reach with one magazine? Today, *The Furrow* has 1.5 million subscribers in 40 countries, according to the John Deere website.

Farming is perhaps the oldest industry, but it remains an innovative part of the economy. *Farm Journal* has covered the agricultural industry since 1877. Beginning in 1952, the magazine began publishing regional editions. In the early 1980s, it began using customer data to segment its audience; each subscriber received a customized magazine based on the region and whether the subscriber was a dairy, corn, or wheat farmer. The May 1984 issue of the magazine had 8,896 unique editions, according to the *Farm Journal* website. Advertisers could take advantage of this segmentation by running their advertisements in the editions delivered to the farmers they wanted to reach.

In the pre-Internet age, no marketers used data with more skill than direct mailers, particularly banks marketing their credit cards. American Express, MasterCard, and Visa used zip codes and demographic data to target their mailings to customers who could use their cards. These brands also used sophisticated A/B testing to measure the relative performance of myriad variables, including envelope size, colors used, and offers. Even an incremental increase in direct response success rates meant millions of dollars to the bottom line of a credit card company.

The Internet gave rise to a new breed of direct marketer, and Dell Inc. was one of the first companies to realize the power of online marketing—and its capability to provide deep insight into the customer. In 1996, Dell entered into e-commerce marketing, constructing its website so consumers could buy computers online. More than simply allowing consumers to order computers via the web, Dell enabled consumers to configure their PCs.

Consumers could specify the amount of storage and RAM, and whether they wanted a CD burner. The process made buying a high-end PC easy, and it put the consumer in control.

The direct-to-consumer marketing provided Dell with keen insight into who its customers were, where they lived, and what they needed. As a result, Dell was able to execute marketing campaigns that targeted past Dell buyers to deliver information and peripherals or upgrades. This direct sales model also gave Dell immediate insight into consumer trends. The company, for instance, had a head start on its competitors who sold via retail outlets on what features consumers were clamoring for in their PCs. This data enabled Dell to be incredibly nimble, maintaining manufacturing inventory for only what customers wanted and to adjust manufacturing to consumer demand on the fly. By 1999, Dell had surpassed Compaq as the number one PC manufacturer in the world.

Russell Fujioka, a former Dell marketing executive and now an executive in residence at Bessemer Venture Partners, said the company developed the same mentality as that of W. Edwards Deming, the famous mid-twentieth-century statistician who reputedly said, “In God we trust; all others must bring data.” Fujioka added, “The reliance on data was very deeply ingrained at Dell.”

But it was in the early 2000s that Amazon.com and Google began using the Internet to take customer focus and the use of data to an entirely new level. These two companies—and others like them—are like data muscles. The more they're used, the stronger their data gets. And the stronger their data gets, the more customer insight they amass. And the more customer insight they amass, the more they're used. It's a virtuous upward spiral for Google and Amazon—and a vicious downward spiral for many of their competitors.

Founded in 1996 by Stanford University graduate students Larry Page and Sergey Brin, Google started as a search engine that “organizes the world's data.” Search engines, such as AltaVista and others, existed before Google. The innovation in Page and

Brin's approach was to rank web pages by the number of inbound links they had, which served as a proxy for the page's level of importance among web users. In effect, they created a huge and automated voting machine, collecting data about what pages users liked the best. This way of delivering search results and serving Internet users was vastly more accurate and an almost instant success.

Page and Brin did not immediately monetize their search engine. However, after some fits and starts, they eventually decided that the most efficient way to generate revenue was to sell search terms through an automated auction called AdWords. Today, prices for search terms can range from a few pennies per click to $142 or more per click for specialized, competitive, and lucrative terms such as *mesothelioma settlement*.

Google is a nearly perfect example of a customer-focused, data-driven company. One of its core tenets is: "Focus on the user and all else will follow." Google's simplicity and speed make the search experience a pleasure for customers.

Marissa Mayer, now the CEO of Yahoo!, used to hold the position of vice president for search products and user experience at Google. Around 2005, customer research indicated that users wanted more search results displayed on the first page: 30 rather than 10. Google ran an experiment, comparing user satisfaction between those receiving 10 search results in 0.4 seconds and those receiving 30 results, which took 0.9 seconds. The results were remarkable. Users getting 30 results searched 20 percent less than those who received 10 results. "As Google gets faster, people search more," Mayer said at a Google I/O conference in 2008, according to a CNET story published at the time, "and as it gets slower, people search less." Blogger Greg Linden wrote about the same phenomenon in a 2006 post, "Marissa Mayer at Web 2.0." He noted that the half-second delay in delivering search results made all the difference. "Half a second delay killed user satisfaction," Linden wrote.

Speed delivers customer satisfaction, and customer satisfaction delivers more searches. Google wants more searches, because the data derived from these searches shows what customers are interested in and allows advertisers to get targeted messages in front of these Google users right when they are ready to buy. It's no wonder that Google generated $59.8 billion in revenue in 2013 and today precompiles and delivers results before the user even hits "search" based on the words being typed in the search box.

With the profits generated from search advertising, Google has acquired the ad networks DoubleClick and YouTube and built the social network Google Plus. With its search engine, ad network, video site, and social network, Google has amassed a 360-degree view of its users and has tremendous stores of data about its users and their interests and preferences. As Google develops its user tracking technology called AdID, it now seems poised to offer advertisers unequaled insight into targeted audiences.

Amazon has placed itself in a similarly powerful position with its combination of data savvy and customer focus. Founded in Seattle, Washington, by Jeff Bezos in 1994, Amazon started as an e-commerce bookseller. The company quickly expanded to offer music, and it now has a wide-ranging e-commerce platform. Amazon is such a customer-focused company that it owns a patent on single-click ordering and strives to make the buying process as simple and painless as possible—even though this customer focus may come at the cost of partner relationships (as its well-publicized dispute with Hachette Book Group indicates) and of employee relations (such as the notoriously stressful conditions in which its warehouse employees toil).

But it is the data that truly sets Amazon apart. Amazon's key data insight is to understand that a buyer's viewing and purchasing history offers insight into what he or she will buy next. By comparing an individual buyer's purchases to those of others who have made similar buys, Amazon developed a recommendation engine that is uncanny in its ability to predict what customers are interested in and, more important, what they will buy next.

Today, you don't have to be an Amazon or a Google to take advantage of big data. Continuing advances in technology have democratized data and made it accessible to virtually every company in the world. And here's just how cheap it is: in the three decades between 1980 and 2009, the cost of a gigabyte of storage plummeted from $193,000 per gigabyte to 7 cents per gigabyte, according to an analysis conducted by software engineer Matthew Komorowski, which he shared in a blog post, "A History of Storage Cost." Faster processing speeds mean data of all kinds can be analyzed quickly. Off-the-shelf marketing stack software and tools—such as marketing automation systems, data management platforms, content management systems, customer relationship management software, and analytics tools—make audience insight via data available to any company willing to make a modest investment.

Big data doesn't mean big expense. Every company is sitting on a goldmine of valuable customer and prospect data—in its e-mail lists, through website interactions, or via its e-commerce data. The key is to find out what's important in this data: to analyze what data points, more than any others, indicate that a prospect is ready to buy or that a customer is ready to upgrade, so that you can take action before any of your competitors do.

CHAPTER 3

The Evolution of the Buyer's Journey, or How the Internet Killed the Three-Martini Lunch

If you've ever watched *Mad Men*, you know Don Draper and his fellow admen used to drink booze at lunch—a lot of booze. This practice had a name: the three-martini lunch.

One reason why this practice thrived and sharing a drink was an accepted part of the workday was that lunch with salespeople was one critical way that businesspeople learned about their industry. It was also how salespeople formed relationships and built trust with the buyers. In those pre-Internet days, buyers had limited avenues for discovering and researching new products. They could read trade magazines and discover new products that way. Monthly publications, such as *Industrial Equipment News* and *New Equipment Digest*, showcased giant inventories of newly introduced products that were essentially rewritten vendor press releases. Buyers could use the reader service cards to get brochures and other content from vendors about their products. The buyers could also attend trade shows where vendors exhibited their products.

And, of course, the potential buyers could go to lunch with salespeople. Over lunch, the salespeople would talk about trends in the sector, pass along industry gossip, discuss their company, and, ultimately, try to win the trust of their potential clients. They did all of this so they could eventually sell the prospect a centrifugal pump, some typewriters, or a heating, ventilation, and air-conditioning (HVAC) system.

When you think about it, those three-martini lunches were the content marketing of the era. Just like content marketing, those lunches were designed to pass along valuable information, to gain the buyer's trust, and, in the end, to sell some product.

So why did the three-martini lunch go by the wayside? Cultural norms changed, for one thing, and getting drunk at lunch (and then driving back to the office) isn't as acceptable as it used to be. Plus, the rise of the Internet ultimately transformed the entire buyer's journey. Buyers who used to rely heavily on salespeople to learn about products could now consult corporate websites, perform Google searches, read product reviews, and solicit the opinions of peers using LinkedIn and other social media before ever contacting a salesperson. The Internet and its various tools of information discovery have forever changed the buyer's journey, giving more control to the buyer and siphoning much of it away from salespeople. In the process, the marketing department—via the data it gathers on a prospect as he or she surfs the web in search of information about a purchase—has gained more influence over the buyer's journey than it ever has had before.

Here's how it happened. In the first phase of the Internet, companies launched corporate websites. They put their company brochures on their sites. Sometimes they put product catalogs and data sheets on their websites, too. Prospects could visit these websites directly, or they could use the first search engines, such as AltaVista, to help them find the products and services they were looking for. But that information was hard to find, and was still largely controlled by the corporation. Salespeople still provided critical details for the buyer during their journey. It wasn't until Google came along and turbocharged search that finding product information online truly got traction. Google revolutionized search for consumers and business-to-business (B2B) buyers by making it fast, simple, and accurate.

Using Google, B2B buyers could, for example, key in the term "centrifugal pump" and find all the information they needed on that product in seconds—without ever having to leave their office. This was step one in deemphasizing the role of the salesperson. Step two was the rise of social media in all its forms, such as blogs and user review sites, as well as Facebook, LinkedIn, and other social networks. Social media led to an explosion of online content, and using tools such as Google and Bing, buyers could find the very specific information they were looking for. Additionally, buyers could now easily locate their peers to find extremely relevant information from trusted and independent sources about the products and services they wanted to buy.

With the growth of search and social media, dramatic changes in the buyer's journey resulted. Salespeople were once involved in almost the entire buyer's journey. They provided background information on industry trends; they gave specific information on the product; they negotiated; they closed the deal.

Now, because of the information power shift to the buyer, the marketing department is the part of the vendor company that is in touch with the buyer throughout the process. Various studies confirm this shift. CEB estimates that the typical B2B prospect is 57 percent of the way through the buyer's journey before contacting a salesperson. Forrester Research found that the potential customer has completed as much as 90 percent of the buyer's journey before reaching out to a salesperson.

What do these numbers mean exactly? A look at changes in the car-buying process can make these statistics about the buyer's journey seem more concrete, because the car-buying process has undergone many of these same changes. Like many B2B products, an automobile is a considered purchase: it is expensive; it generally involves research by the prospective buyer; it is a purchase expected to last and perform for several years; and it tends to involve a buying team (in the case of a car, Mom, Dad, and the kids, rather than the CIO, CFO, and a handful of middle managers for B2B purchases).

In the past, the information in the car-buying process was asymmetrical. The salesperson, by far, had most of the information. Prospective car buyers could consult *Consumer Reports* or the guy down the street who could repair the engine on his GTO, but the car-buying process didn't truly start until the buyer walked into the car dealership. And the car dealership was the car salesperson's turf. The salesperson knew the wholesale value of the car, had access to what other buyers had paid, knew how well—or poorly—the car model was performing, and knew how happy—or unhappy—previous buyers of the car model were. The prospective buyer had access to the car's sticker price, and that was about it.

In the digital age, however, the prospective car buyer has easy access to information once available to only the salesperson at the dealership. Online, prospects can find the wholesale price of the car they are considering; they can discover what previous buyers have paid for similar models or even for the exact car they are considering; and they know, through product review sites, how owners feel about the car's performance. They even know that the same exact car is available a few towns away and at a better price. Buyers now have data that puts them on equal footing with the car salesperson; the information is no longer asymmetrical. And by the time buyers walk into a dealership, they know the model they want and often exactly what they want to pay. By the time a buyer comes face-to-face with a salesperson, the buying process is essentially over except for some minor haggling and signing the documents.

The evolution of the *Kelley Blue Book* from an information source reserved for dealers to a free website aimed at consumers is emblematic of the shift in data availability. The *Kelley Blue Book*, which is the de facto pricing guide for used cars, was started almost by accident by a California car dealer named Les Kelley, according to a history of the *Kelley Blue Book* published on the KBB.com website. An expert at repairing and restoring cars, Kelley used his skills to create what was at one time the largest car dealership in the United States back in the early part of the twentieth century. To other dealers, Kelley distributed a list of the used cars he was interested in buying and the prices he would pay for them. Kelley's list became widely trusted as the barometer for wholesale used car pricing.

Ever the entrepreneur, Kelley saw an opportunity and began publishing his list as the *Kelley Blue Book*, a reference to the Cleveland Social Directory, also known as the "Cleveland Blue Book," which listed the prominent society families in Cleveland. Kelley published his first book in 1926, and his publishing business quickly became a bigger revenue producer than his car dealerships. For decades, Kelley sold the book exclusively to other businesses—mainly dealerships, car insurance companies, and banks that made car loans. It wasn't until 1993 that the first print edition of the *Kelley Blue Book* was published, aimed at consumers. Two years later, information from the *Kelley Blue Book* made its first appearance online at KBB.com. Kelley initially charged consumers $3.95 for a report, but within weeks stopped charging consumers, made the information free, and adopted an advertising model to support the site. The end result was a big first step in leveling the playing field in the car-buying process by offering consumers access to the same information that dealers had been privy to for decades.

A similar evolution has happened in the B2B buying world. Prospects research their potential purchases online, using Google to find product data, visiting product review sites, and soliciting peer opinions on social media. By the time the B2B buyer reaches out to the salesperson, there is often little to be learned. The salesperson is perhaps there to negotiate some terms and take the order.

But even if the salesperson is in contact with prospects much later in the buyer's journey, the marketing department has a window on buyer behavior much earlier in the process—if they are looking. Marketers can observe how prospects are visiting their website, responding to e-mail, interacting with social media, and behaving after viewing online display or search engine advertising. Steve Woods, former CTO of Eloqua and current CTO of Nudge, called this process of gauging a prospective buyer's search history and online behavior "digital body language." In his book *Digital Body Language* (New Year Publishing, 2010), Woods wrote, "A sales professional's ability to observe and understand the buyer's body language was an irreplaceable component of his success. That's no longer possible in the new paradigm. Instead, marketers must rise to the challenges: marketers must cultivate new skills to observe and understand the buyer's digital body language."

And like salespeople, marketers can adjust their actions based on a prospect's digital body language. For instance, a marketer can target prospects with tailored display ads based on what part of the marketer's website they visited or what previous display ads they've viewed (a technique called *retargeting*). A marketer can follow up with the offer of a discount if a prospect opened a specific e-mail. Marketers can also reach out to their Facebook "likes" or Twitter followers with suggestions on what content to download, what white papers to read, or what videos to watch—across millions of interactions—in a completely automated manner.

When prospects raised their hands to show their interest in a particular company's product or service, it used to be the salesperson who did the talking, supplying the content and interacting with the customer. Now, however, when the prospect visits a website or otherwise offers digital signals of interest in a company's product or service, the forward-thinking marketing team automatically directs the prospect to the appropriate online content. For instance, if prospects visit the website, they may be directed to a white paper. If they read an e-mail, they might receive a follow-up e-mail with a discounted offer. If they click on a search ad, they could be retargeted with a gated content offer trying to get contact information. Only if they become a marketing qualified lead (MQL) do they get handed off to the sales team to try to touch base in a human-to-human interaction.

Content produced by the marketing team has always played a role in educating buyers, long before the Internet. In the days before digital, marketers produced brochures and industrial videos that the sales team could use as calling cards. In the early days of Google, digital content—often in the form of blogs or web pages—quickly became more important, because content, especially good content that generated a lot of hyperlinks and was a powerful search engine optimization (SEO) tool for Google's algorithm, was a critical way that a website could earn a high ranking on Google's search results. Having gated content (content that prospects would share their e-mail addresses to read) became critical to generating leads.

Every interaction that prospects have with a potential vendor's website, social media pages, or online advertising creates data. It is this data—the big data—that Woods refers to as the potential buyer's digital body language. Some marketers see prospects creating millions of data points every month, every week, or even every day. To track this data and ensure that they are processing it correctly and ultimately interacting with prospects in the proper way online and offline, marketers are installing arsenals of software that can include marketing automation systems, customer relationship management software, data management platforms, analytics tools, and content management systems.

This software is called the marketing technology stack. And the ability to implement it properly, use it effectively, and integrate all the pieces together efficiently is what will separate the great companies from their competition.

CHAPTER 4

The Marketing Stack—Why CMOs and CIOs Are Working Together

Marketing automation software. Customer relationship management (CRM) systems. Data management platforms. Analytics tools. These are the weapons in a marketing arms race; these are the technologies that provide marketers with the data they need to gather insights into their customers and prospects and to measure the impact of their marketing programs. When these technologies are integrated together in what is called the marketing technology stack, the data they generate can be even more powerful.

The elements of the marketing technology stack enable marketers to see what their prospects and customers are doing online, to read their digital body language. With the transformative changes to the buyer's journey, these software programs are the radar and the night-vision goggles of the marketing world, tools that allow marketers to see their targets in conditions where before they could see very little.

In this new era, having a data-driven CMO who understands IT is critical to success. That's because marketers need technology to be able to collect and process the data that helps them target prospects, communicate with customers, and measure marketing program performance. Motorola Solutions believes that IT is so crucial to marketing success that Eduardo Conrado, who holds the title of senior vice president of marketing and IT, oversees both departments.

To take advantage of data, marketers must now understand IT or at least work hand-in-hand with the department. "Stepping Up to the Challenge: CMO Insights from the Global C-Suite Study," a 2014 study by IBM, concluded: "Where the CMO and the CIO work well together, the enterprise is 76 percent more likely to outperform in terms of revenue and profitability."

Like many marketing executives today, Nick Panayi, director of global brand and digital marketing at information technology (IT) and professional services firm Computer Sciences Corporation (CSC), strives to have a good working relationship with his company's IT department. Marketing teams more than ever depend on technology and software, which is why it is vital that you have a working relationship with IT—and that your marketing staff is tech-savvy.

"I think there's value in partnering with IT, while maintaining marketing tech experts within marketing," he said.

Marketing needs to be more nimble than a traditional IT department, which, in the past, has moved cautiously in adopting new systems. "Marketing technology moves way too fast," Panayi said.

When he joined CSC, he made the marketing stack his first priority. Panayi explained: "The CIO of the organization was not at all familiar or comfortable making decisions around marketing automation platforms, redesigning the website, looking at the CMS, looking at the analytics and predictive models. They are plenty smart; they just didn't have the ability or the interest at that point in time. So they basically said, 'Listen, we need you to make the decision on what marketing platforms and what analytics platform and how you tie that all together to the CRM system. We'll do it with you, but we need you to take the business lead and we need you to guide it.' It has continued ever since to be a very strong, symbiotic relationship, but it started right at the beginning."

As part of his relationship with IT, Panayi has a number of technology-focused staffers on his team. In today's marketing department, it's absolutely necessary to have this skill set.

Because of the growing imperative of marketing technology, the marketing team at CSC comprises three main personnel components—infrastructure, content marketing, and demand generation—all of which use various types of software in the marketing stack. The people working in infrastructure are adept at implementing software and analyzing data. The demand generation team runs marketing automation software such as Eloqua or Marketo. And even the content creators must be adept with their blogging platform and analyzing data on how their content is performing.

Robert Davis, executive vice president at PJA Marketing + Advertising, is an admirer of CSC's approach to integrating marketing and technology. "I was blown away by CSC's implementation and the way they have changed their business process around a completely integrated stack, because its technology is integrated with process in a way that is really impressive," Davis said.

As the marketing team at CSC illustrates, the composition of the marketing department is changing, because marketers must now also be well versed in how to use a myriad of software programs and platforms to reach and track the behavior of their customers and prospects across the web. To install, run, and integrate these software programs, marketing departments require marketing automation specialists and software developers. Some companies are hiring chief marketing technologists, a position described as the CIO of the marketing department. A Gartner study by Laura McLellan, in fact, found that 81 percent of large companies have a chief marketing technologist on staff.

As you might expect from the man who is the author of the *Chief Marketing Technologist* blog, Scott Brinker asserts that the chief marketing technologist role "is incredibly critical. Almost all of the interactions and touch points that marketing has with prospective customers are mediated through software. The customer-centric nature of these technologies goes far beyond traditional marketing. These touch points orchestrated by marketing software are the engine of a front-facing customer experience. This is becoming part of the operating system within your organization as a whole. It connects into sales; it connects into customer service; and it connects into how we are evolving our product and service delivery lines. Companies still need an IT function serving as the centralized governance authority and managing centralized infrastructure. But at the same time, marketing must proactively synthesize technology into strategy and operations—to really understand how to apply technology in the service of brilliant marketing. And that's where these marketing technologists shine:

bridging marketing and IT and helping them collaborate more effectively."

In conjunction with the marketing technologist role becoming more common, Gartner's McLellan also predicted that marketers are ramping up their spending on software so quickly that CMOs would spend more than CIOs on information technology by 2017. But some observers say it's difficult to differentiate what marketing is spending on technology and what IT is spending on technology. In the most effective companies the two departments are investing together in software for the good of the overall business.

It's easy to say that marketing and IT must work together; it's far harder to do. Marketing and technology have some lingering barriers to overcome. Chief among these barriers may be their different pace of operation and their different definitions of speed. Marketing is necessarily quick, looking to move fast to take advantage of market shifts. Marketing wants new technologies and software installed quickly, and the cloud and software as a service (SaaS) have made this desire a reality. IT, in contrast, has traditionally been more cautious, waiting to install new technologies until it's clear they have become or are going to become the standard.

"IT tends to think in six-month or one-year increments, and marketers—at the outside—are thinking in time frames of quarters, because that's how they're measured," Davis said.

"Marketing—and especially digital marketing—moves at the speed of the Internet," Panayi said. "It moves in a flash. There's too much going on. By the time you stop and think about it a little too long, you've missed the opportunity to participate, whether it's a new social media channel or a new ad technology or something like that. It's important for you to work relatively quickly and adjust your system to what's going on in digital marketing. IT is not designed that way. IT is designed to be a risk-averse organization. It is not designed to be at the edge of innovation or at the edge of technology changes. It's designed to really take something and make sure it's battle-tested and bulletproof before deciding to fully deploy it. In the world of marketing technology, that's not fast enough. If you fail, you 'fail fast' and move on, since many times the risk of not participating is higher than the risk of making a mistake. So what we've tried to do is straddle those two worlds, and we have an organization that reflects that relationship and has learned to keep an optimal balance."

The best organizations are those where IT and marketing work together and work out their differences at a reasonable speed. And it's not just about marketing and IT working together. It's about sales, finance, manufacturing, product development—all of these elements cooperating. "Leaders within companies are people who are able to manifest this multifunctional perspective," Davis said. "This isn't something marketing is going to do on its own; this is something we're going to do as an organization, and it's going to be the engine that drives our business moving forward."

Consulting firm McKinsey & Company published an article in August 2014, "Getting the CMO and CIO to Work as Partners," that explored elements of this topic. Here is how the article's authors, Matt Ariker, Martin Harrysson, and Jesko Perrey, described how businesses must adapt to a world overflowing with software and teeming with the data it produces: "Both the CMO and CIO are on the hook for turning all that data into growth together. It may be a marriage of convenience, but it's one that CMOs and CIOs need to make work, especially as worldwide volume of data is growing at least 40 percent a year, with ever-increasing variety and velocity."

The McKinsey article offered several tips for solidifying the CMO-CIO relationship:

Set well-defined goals, together. As the authors wrote, "When you're looking for a needle in a haystack of big data, you really need to know what a needle looks like." With a specific and shared target in mind, the marketing and IT teams will be forced to work together. Marketing and IT must share accountability to get the job done right.

The CMO must become metrics driven and transparent. In addition to having clear goals, the CMO must choose the right metrics for gauging the outcomes of the use of technology and the data it produces. These metrics must be shared and completely transparent so the team—both the marketing and IT departments—can understand their progress toward meeting the ultimate goals.

The CIO must shift mind-set. For too long, IT has been a cost center. The CIO must now approach the business as a unit that will accelerate revenue, McKinsey says.

Team building is essential. One way to get marketers and IT folks to work together is to hire people who have a keen understanding of both. The authors of this article suggest hiring "marketing and IT translators."

Think big but start small. Data—big, small, and otherwise—can be a complex undertaking. McKinsey counsels starting small with a pilot program or two. The advice is to "fail fast" and identify sticking points quickly to make the current project better, and future projects even better than that.

At Dun & Bradstreet Credibility Corporation, Aaron Stibel, the company's senior vice president of technology, has been implementing, along with the rest of the management team, many of the steps recommended by McKinsey.

"Marketing and technology, we operate as one team," Stibel said. "In fact, we sit out in the open at big tables all together. On any given day, if you walked back here, you might not be able to tell the difference between the marketing team and the technology team. That's how closely aligned we are. Even our project management meetings are all run with marketing and technology together. . . . You wouldn't think so, but the physical move together is quite important."

D&B Credibility has also brought together all of the company's data in one place, where all departments have easy access to it. "We've centralized the whole data silo within technology," Stibel said. "We work very closely with our internal partners. The problem was multiple sources of 'truth' all over the company. So when we started afresh, we said, 'Let's centralize data across all of its users and all of its customers.'"

D&B Credibility revamped its technology backbone in 2012 and 2013 with a project called Phoenix. The company-wide project "transformed and integrated the existing technology platforms from several expensive legacy systems into a single platform utilizing SaaS, cloud, and open-source technologies." With the new IT infrastructure, they boosted their product fulfillment, CRM, data warehousing, and business intelligence capabilities. Additionally, in conjunction with marketing, the new Phoenix infrastructure enabled the launch of 13 new products.

Stibel is proud to say that the Phoenix project was recognized by *CIO* magazine with a CIO 100 Award in 2013 for "strategic excellence in information technology." Stibel said, "This is not a technology award. It's an award for the entire company."

This holistic view of the business is what has changed not only how marketing and IT operate, but how the entire company operates, Stibel said. "In a lot of organizations, IT is in charge of shuffling laptops around, getting things working, and every once in a while spearheading a project," he added. "But with true, fast-moving product companies, there just can't be a difference between marketing and technology. They just have to be the same."

Companies with marketers who are focused on marketing technology and on installing and taking full advantage of these platforms will have an advantage over competitors that have not fully embraced technology, and will have a clearer picture of their customers' wants, their pain points, and their needs. The early adopters of these marketing technologies are moving far beyond the simple installation and usage of these software programs; they are integrating these platforms together in an effort to build a unified, 360-degree view of the customer. The area where many marketers are seeing the first fruits of this integration is in linking their marketing automation software with their CRM platforms to bridge what has historically been a large gap—sometimes even a yawning canyon—between sales and marketing.

The Big Business of Selling Software to Marketers

As businesses spend more on marketing technology, companies like Adobe, Google, IBM, Oracle, Salesforce.com, and SAP are acquiring and developing new software and systems enabling them to offer more and increasingly sophisticated software to the marketing team. This new focus on technology and marketing has led to a series of significant acquisitions and changes made by some of the top software giants.

Adobe

Adobe was originally founded in 1982 to develop the PostScript page description language, which helped make desktop publishing possible. Over the past decade, Adobe has increasingly moved to serve the entire marketing department, from the creative side to the technology side. The company has made many acquisitions—such as Aldus, the creator of PageMaker, in 1994, and Photoshop the following year—that targeted the creative portion of the marketing team.

In 2014, Adobe introduced an upgraded version of the Adobe Marketing Cloud, a product that integrates media optimization, social, web experience, content management, campaign management, and analytics. Adobe also announced a deal that made SAP, which has been less aggressive than its competitors in moving into marketing technology, a global reseller of the Adobe Marketing Cloud. As part of this deal, the Adobe Marketing Cloud is also being integrated into SAP's HANA platform and its Hybris Commerce Suite.

Among Adobe's major marketing software acquisitions are:

2009: Omniture, web analytics, $1.8 billion
2011: Demdex, data management platform, $58 million
2011: Auditude, video ad platform, $120 million
2011: Efficient Frontier, programmatic search marketing platform, $400 million
2014: Neolane, marketing automation software, $600 million

Google

Google, of course, got its start with search. The company is synonymous with search, but as a business it has moved far beyond that corner of digital advertising to embrace a large swath of digital marketing. Google has used the vast profits from its search engine advertising business to acquire more than 150 businesses that built its data-driven digital marketing offerings. Some of Google's acquisitions are:

2006: YouTube, online video platform, $1.65 billion
2007: DoubleClick, ad server and advertising exchange, $3.1 billion
2009: AdMob, mobile ad network, $750 million

2009: Teracent, dynamic ad platform, ~$40 million
2010: Invite Media, demand-side platform, ~$85 million
2011: AdMeld, supply-side platform, $400 million
2012: Motorola Mobility, mobile devices and software, $2.9 billion
2014: Spider.io, anti–ad fraud detection, undisclosed
2014: Nest, smart thermostat maker, $3.2 billion

IBM

IBM has shown an enviable capability to change with the times. The one-time business machine company is now itself a business machine. In one of its iterations, IBM essentially invented the position of the CIO and sold American and international business on the value of computing. In the 1990s, Lou Gerstner took the helm of IBM and turned a struggling hardware company into a consulting business. Now IBM has turned its sights on selling the CMO and the marketing team on the power of technology. Much of IBM's analytics business, which has been built primarily via acquisition with a war chest of billions, included deals like the following designed to build a product set attractive to marketers:

2007: Cognos, business intelligence platform, $4.9 billion
2009: SPSS, business analytics, $1.2 billion
2010: Coremetrics, web analytics, $240 million
2010: Unica, customer preference software, $480 million
2010: Sterling Commerce, business-to-business (B2B) e-commerce, $1.6 billion

Microsoft

Microsoft has had an inconsistent relationship with the marketing department. On one hand, its MSN portal has been a mainstay of digital advertising for years. However, Microsoft's $6 billion acquisition of aQuantive in 2007 has been judged a disaster. Additionally, it sold the Atlas advertising platform, a part of aQuantive, to Facebook. Microsoft does offer the Microsoft Dynamics CRM system, which is an offshoot of the Microsoft Dynamics ERP enterprise resource planning system, which was built via acquisition of software companies such as Great Plains. Microsoft eventually wrote off the lion's share of the aQuantive deal.

Oracle

While IBM first entered businesses through the CIO, Oracle came in through the CFO. Now both are going after the budgets of the increasingly deep-pocketed CMO. As befits its leader, Larry Ellison, Oracle has been an extremely aggressive acquirer of late of businesses aimed at serving the marketing department. Some key acquisitions for the Oracle Marketing Cloud:

2012: Vitrue, social media management platform, $300 million
2012: Involver, social media development platform, ~$20 million
2012: Eloqua, marketing automation software, $810 million
2013: Compendium, blogging platform, undisclosed
2013: Responsys, marketing automation software, $1.5 billion
2014: BlueKai, data management platform, $400 million

Salesforce.com

As its name suggests, Salesforce.com is primarily aimed at the sales team with its core product, a software-as-a-service customer relationship management tool. But these days, integration of CRM systems with marketing automation software has brought the sales team and marketing closer together. Salesforce.com is looking to leverage this trend by acquiring more technology it can sell to the marketing department. Among its highest-profile acquisitions are:

2010: Jigsaw, crowdsourced business database, $142 million
2011: Radian6, social media software, $326 million
2012: Buddy Media, social media software, $689 million
2013: ExactTarget, marketing automation software, $2.5 billion

SAP

Among the software giants, SAP has made the fewest moves to court the marketing team. SAP did acquire Hybris, an e-commerce platform—and e-commerce is increasingly being viewed as marketing's responsibility. Additionally, SAP reached an agreement in 2014 to be a global reseller for the Adobe Marketing Cloud.

The Software in the Stack

As the sidebar, "The Big Business of Selling Software to Marketers," makes clear, the software giants have collectively spent billions to go after CMO budgets. But they are not alone in targeting the marketing department. There are countless marketing technology and advertising technology start-ups going after marketing dollars. Led by tech sector CMOs, marketers are embracing marketing technology software to varying degrees. Because the technology is often delivered in the cloud as a software as a service (SaaS) offering, most marketing software—in one form or another—is accessible for businesses of all sizes and budgets.

Not all marketers are using marketing technology in the same way, but trends and best practices are emerging for taking full advantage of data to gently drive prospects through the marketing funnel and to provide personalized service to customers. Here's a cross section of the marketing technology software—the elements that together make up the marketing stack—that are gaining traction.

Marketing Automation Software

For many marketers, their marketing automation software is the centerpiece of the marketing stack. The leading brands in the arena are ExactTarget, Marketo, and Oracle | Eloqua. For now, many marketers use their marketing automation software as a glorified e-mail newsletter platform, but these platforms can do much more. Using marketing automation systems, marketers can segment their audience by company size, industry, job title, and other key data points. Using this data, marketers can then deliver to these segments precise nurture flows to drive them to relevant content. Marketing automation systems can also implement lead scoring programs that help marketers send only the most qualified leads to sales (and the sales team's CRM systems).

Business Intelligence Databases

These products, which are provided by IBM, Oracle, SAP, Tableau Software, Domo, and many others, allow companies to analyze their big data and derive insights about what's working and what's not. These software packages allow businesses to create dashboards, charts, and other visualizations for easy analysis of data.

For instance, a marketing team can use this kind of software to create dashboards that track leads, sales opportunities, and revenue generated by marketing qualified leads.

CRM Systems

Customer relationship management systems, such as those provided by Microsoft Dynamics, Oracle, Salesforce.com, NetSuite, and SAP, are typically deployed and used by sales and account management teams as their customer systems-of-record. Like business intelligence software, CRM systems provide dashboards that allow sales chiefs to quickly see the sales pipeline, number of leads, deals closed, and other critical data. For the individual salespeople, the system allows account and contact management and enables them to track their activities against their pipeline of accounts. Leading CMOs integrate their marketing automation software with CRM systems, and, when done properly, this integration can help improve communication between sales and marketing regarding lead generation, lead qualification, and marketing-sourced deals.

Content Management Systems

For most marketers, a content management system (CMS) allows fast and easy posting and changing of content on the corporate website. The best systems allow designers and content producers to post, replace, and correct text, images, and videos without relying on the information technology department to dot every *I* and cross every *T*. The best content management systems take a change on, for example, a website and then allow users to instantly make that change elsewhere, such as in catalogs or on mobile pages. Additionally, the most useful CMSs tap into data to automatically serve relevant content based on a user's previous visits or demographic or business demographic information, such as geolocation, industry, or job title, contained in their cookie. Leaders in this arena included Adobe, OpenText, Oracle, and SiteCore.

Blogging Platforms

Content marketing is critical to attracting prospects and customers to a marketer's website. For content marketers, there is a range of blogging and general-purpose content publishing platforms such as Glam Media's Ning, Moveable Type, Oracle's Compendium, and WordPress. These platforms stress ease of use, both for designing templates and for day-to-day content creation. Beyond this ease of use, these blogging platforms are designed to push out content—via e-mail newsletter, search engine optimization aids, and RSS feeds—to your target audience. The best blogging platforms also provide easily accessible data on readership, traffic, and time spent on individual posts.

Data Management Platforms

Adobe, Aggregate Knowledge, BlueKai (acquired by Oracle), CoreAudience, Krux, and Lotame are the leading data management platforms (DMPs). A DMP uses first-party and third-party cookies as well as application programming interfaces (APIs) to create audience segments that marketers can then target with their online advertising. Using this data, marketers can measure the performance of their ads targeting these audience segments and optimize them to improve performance.

Analytics Tools

Analytics tools provide a data-driven window into a marketer's web traffic. These tools offer insight into where users come from, what search terms or ads are driving website traffic, what pages are sticky, and where visitors are exiting the site. Analytics leaders include Adobe Web Analytics, Chartbeat, Google Analytics (which is free for sites generating fewer than 10 million monthly hits), KISSmetrics, and Mint.

Social Media Management Software

Social media management software is available in a variety of shapes and sizes. Many software products help with a range of objectives that can include social listening, post scheduling, social selling, customer care, analytics, curation, and promotion. This software can use data to help marketers discern what kind of posts and which social networks are delivering the most traffic and conversions. Among the leading social software brands are Adobe Social, Buddy Media/Radian6/Salesforce, HootSuite, Vitrue/Oracle, Sprinklr, Sprout Social, TweetDeck, Viralheat, and WebTrends.

Predictive Lead Scoring

Predictive lead scoring vendors, such as FlipTop, Infer, KXEN (an SAP company), and Lattice Engines, use big data to help marketers and sales teams identify the best sales leads. Predictive lead scoring engines perform a statistical analysis on the best-performing leads with the goal of determining what hundreds or thousands of factors are the best predictors of success. For instance, is the size of the company or what medium generated the lead a better predictor of success than whether the lead's company is preparing for an initial public offering (IPO) or just moved to new office space?

Customer Service/Call Center Software

Customer service software, such as Freshdesk, inContact, Team-Support, and Zendesk, enable support to help call centers answer customer questions and solve customer problems as easily and as quickly as possible. The best systems tap into a unified customer database, so that the employees on the front lines have easy access to customer history—including both offline and online interactions—so that, for instance, the call center worker isn't asking questions that the database already has the answer to.

E-Commerce Platforms

Among the leading enterprise e-commerce platforms are IBM WebSphere, Oracle ATG, and SAP's Hybris. E-commerce platforms straddle the divide between marketing and sales. No matter which department controls this function, the data derived by delving into sales patterns is invaluable to understanding who are buying, what they're buying, and how much they're spending. E-commerce also offers tremendous marketing opportunities to up-sell and cross-sell customers. The capability to suggest other products either on the spot or in subsequent e-mails gives marketers the opportunity to make sure customers buy ancillary products from you and not from your competitors.

Search Engine Management Platforms

SEM platforms are designed to help marketers manage, automate, and optimize their search engine marketing and pay-per-click campaigns. The most sophisticated platforms enable marketers to develop intelligent bid strategies, optimize creative, identify the most effective keywords, and provide analytics to measure performance. These platforms use data and attribution to allow marketers to measure cross-channel performance among display, mobile, search, and social compaigns. Among the more recognizable platforms are Kenshoo and Marin Software.

Demand-Side Platform (DSP)

A demand-side platform (DSP) is a software platform that enables marketers and their agencies to use real-time bidding (RTB) on multiple online advertising exchanges to purchase display ads across thousands of online publishers. Using RTB, which is an electronic bidding process akin to the way stocks are sold on the New York Stock Exchange or NASDAQ, the DSP allows marketers to bid on ad impressions based on their desire (or lack of desire) to reach an individual web visitor based on his or her demographics, online behavior, or both. With RTB, DSPs provide marketers an automated, centralized, and scaled approach to audience targeting—and the transactions take milliseconds, occurring billions of times a day across the Internet. Among the leading DSPs are MediaMath and Turn. Supply-side platforms (SSP) are similar to DSPs; the key difference is that an SSP is designed for the supply side of the ad-buying equation—the online publishers—to maximize their price per impression. AppNexus is a leading SSP.

CHAPTER 5

How Technology Bridges the Gap between Marketing and Sales

Glengarry Glen Ross, the 1992 film based on David Mamet's play, is a cult classic among salespeople. There are a handful of great lines from the movie that are routinely quoted in sales meetings or whenever salespeople gather together all over the world.

"Third prize is you're fired."

"That watch costs more than your car."

"A-B-C—Always be closing."

And of course: "Coffee's for closers."

In addition to being one of the best films ever about the often intensely competitive environment of sales, a key element in the plot of *Glengarry Glen Ross* is sales leads. The salesmen complain that the leads they have been getting to sell real estate are weak. The significance of leads is conveyed through the two story lines: one of the salesmen actually steals the leads from a locked vault, and one of the leads thought to be a sure sale turns out to be a couple who have no money to purchase the real estate—they just want the company of a salesperson.

As in the movie, leads are often at the heart of the relationship between sales and marketing, a relationship that has historically been rocky—many times on account of disputes over the value of leads. Salespeople, as they do in *Glengarry Glen Ross*, often find that leads from marketing leave something to be desired. Marketing, in turn, feels that the salespeople fail to follow up on the quality leads supplied to them.

In this digital age, the sales and marketing teams at many companies are working more closely together, and the fundamental changes in the buyer's journey and the capabilities of the marketing technology stack are part of the reason. With smarter use of data, marketing is delivering better leads, which means salespeople are more effectively closing deals. If salespeople are closing more deals, it means the sales department begins to have more trust in marketing's leads and so pays more attention to them. It also means that there's more revenue, which creates harmony between sales and marketing—and pretty much everyone in the company.

Nick Panayi, who started at Computer Sciences Corporation (CSC) in 2011 as director of global brand and digital marketing, has focused on building a relationship of trust between sales and marketing, and marketing technology has been a critical part in building that trust. "Marketing and sales have always been in this interesting relationship, a marriage of convenience almost," he said. "Marketing obviously needs sales to be able to provide value to the business. Sales needs marketing to be able to take some time to basically broaden and accelerate their funnel. But it's always been a difficult relationship, and marketing has been in a fight for relevance for a long time, I would say.

"What's different nowadays is that there is plenty of research that has shed light on the buyer's journey. The fact is that—pick your percentage from 60 to 70 to 80 percent, depending on which study you believe—a big part of the buyer's journey, from glimmer in the prospect's eye to the signing of the check, is digital. So as a sales professional, whether you truly appreciate marketing or not, the very basic fact that marketing is the only entity in the company that can shed light on that 60 percent to 80 percent of what the buyer did before talking to you ought to be enough for you to pay attention."

To have a deep and relevant view of that critical portion of the buyer's journey that takes place online, a marketer needs tools. A marketer needs a technology stack. When Panayi joined CSC, the company didn't have the tools he wanted.

"When we started, we really had nothing. There was no marketing database, no marketing automation platform," Panayi said. "The website looked like it was from the 1980s. There was no marketing ecosystem per se."

So, working with CSC's IT department, Panayi built a modern system essentially from scratch. He designed the stack so that marketing could understand the needs of customers and prospects, support sales, and ultimately drive revenue. Panayi now calls it the "leads-to-cash" ecosystem.

At the foundation is a content management system. "This is a system that is very flexible and very modular," he said. "It allows us to have very rapid adaption of new technology."

The marketing automation software is Oracle | Eloqua. The analytics platform had been Adobe—the Omniture piece, in particular—but CSC recently acquired InfoChimps, and is building up its big data capabilities using that platform to eat its own dog food. "We will, in essence, be customer zero for that platform," Panayi said. "We'll be adopting our own technologies for more advanced analytics and predictive modeling techniques."

These software platforms are the core of CSC's marketing stack, which Panayi estimates has more than 50 distinct elements, when everything from databases and webinar platforms is accounted for. The stack, particularly the Eloqua piece, is integrated with the sales team's customer relationship management (CRM) system, which is Salesforce.com.

To feed the Salesforce.com platform the leads it craves, CSC has developed a data-based system of evaluating leads that is both automated and touched by human hands. Panayi said the leads process has many filters—agreed upon by sales and marketing—before leads are passed along to sales. "We have built rigor into the whole lead qualification and leads-to-cash process," he said.

CSC used to have more than 100 various "contact us" forms on its website that delivered leads to different parts of the business. Panayi has streamlined that system so that all leads are processed via Eloqua. "It's now one form, a template with a couple of variations for simple and more complex interactions," he said. "On Eloqua there are automated rules that immediately strip out roughly 60 percent of 'leads' that are not really leads. Job seekers, organizations that are looking to do partnerships with the company, smaller companies that are looking to sell us tools or whatever it may be; we're able, with automated rules, to understand whether or not this is a customer in our target set—whether they are large enough or not and whether they are truly interested in something we can serve them. So those rules are able to strip away all of those needs that would otherwise go to the sales organization. Only the ones that are MLs, or marketing leads, get escalated to Salesforce."

After the Eloqua software uses data to determine what leads qualify as marketing leads, human hands get involved in the process. CSC uses an inside sales team or sales development reps (CSC calls them telequalification agents) to vet the leads via phone calls and e-mails. "If they are new prospects, they go into a holding tank. The telequalification group basically does as many as five attempts to gather advance criteria on the prospect, and only the ones that pass the advance test get passed on to sales."

And the lead is not simply passed on to sales. It is passed on to sales surrounded by data.

"Using Salesforce, the salesperson is able to see where this person has been on the website, if they have answered any e-mails or not, what e-mails they were sent. All this information is available. So not only do we introduce two filters, we only give sales the best of the best leads. We also give them leads that eliminate the need for them to go back and figure out what this lead is all about before they get on the phone with the customer. They also have a pretty comprehensive write-up from the telequalification agent, and we also have the digital footsteps that, in essence, surround that prospect inside Salesforce."

For large customers, CSC's marketing team deploys what it calls account-based marketing. The account-based marketing squad keeps tabs on big companies and government agencies that are CSC's bread and butter. Using a data-driven platform, these teams track the social media activity, statements in the press, and appearances at events of the executives at companies and organizations targeted by CSC.

"They gather this information together," Panayi explained, "and they sift through the mass of contents to look for the needle in the haystack that says, 'Hey, we have a commercial insight here. There is something going on that I can triangulate between what the executive is saying, what the company is saying publicly, and what I know from our sales organization.' . . . This is a bridge between our sales organization and marketing. In this case, what we did to sales is not, 'Hey, check out this Google news story of what your account said.' It's significantly deeper than that, because it says, 'Check out what they said, and, look, this is supported by those executives on what they said, and, by the way, this seems to map very nicely to what you guys said you want to do with this account in the next six months.'"

This method of tracking accounts is part of how CSC puts the philosophy of the Challenger Sale into action. This methodology is based on the book by Matthew Dixon and Brent Adamson, *The Challenger Sale: Taking Control of the Customer Conversation* (Portfolio, 2011). This book argues that the best salespeople challenge conventional ways of thinking and bring their customers new ideas. They don't simply ask customers what they want and then say their company delivers that solution. Any salesperson can do that. Dixon and Adamson write, "Customers have been demanding more depth and expertise. They expect salespeople to teach them things they don't know. These are the core skills of Challengers. They are the skills of the future."

At CSC, the marketing efforts support the sales team by finding commercial insights that can help position the company as a solution different from what others in the market are offering. In addition to the commercial insights, the marketing team steps in and uses data to build extremely targeted and customized communications plans for sales.

Marketing, Panayi says, "provides the ability to basically bring to sales just-in-time campaigns—tactics that make sense for that insight. So instead of going to sales and saying, 'Hey, let me tell you about these 15 campaigns we have running and everything about our social media presence,' they basically walk in and say, 'Here's the commercial insight, and if we all agree this is valid, here are two campaigns that are going on that I can take and customize. And, by the way, we're going to build a mini social media campaign and go after these five individuals with LinkedIn messages.' So it is, in essence, a just-in-time marketing plan, tailor-made for that account.

"That's real value."

Technology Brings Harmony between Sales and Marketing at DocuSign

Meagen Eisenberg is vice president of customer marketing at DocuSign, which provides digital transaction management solutions. DocuSign is a great example of a company that is embracing digital marketing technology. The company has a robust marketing technology stack, and has perhaps even more robust results to show for it. Eisenberg previously held marketing roles at Hewlett-Packard (HP), Cisco, and IBM. For her, the relationship between marketing and sales is critical. "I've gone to many companies where that relationship wasn't there, and the first thing I worked on was building it," Eisenberg said.

Driving leads that are based on data is central to the way this relationship is constructed. A critical piece of driving leads and the DocuSign marketing stack is the Eloqua marketing automation platform. Eisenberg says that DocuSign generates about 130,000 leads a quarter, or more than 40,000 per month, and the sales team has the capacity to handle only about 20 percent of the total leads, or about 8,000 per month. So it's essential that the DocuSign marketing team deliver to the sales staff the leads most likely to develop into a deal.

"It's so important that I am accurately depicting which ones they should call and which ones they should not call first," Eisenberg says. "What if they call the 20 percent that doesn't convert? And now the ones that would've converted never heard from us and then the lead is left to die? It's a huge thing about leveraging that data to make sales more efficient."

Eloqua, with its lead scoring capability, has been the cornerstone of DocuSign's efforts to give sales not only a lot of leads, but also the right leads. Eisenberg was very satisfied with the results. "We get the importance of scoring," she said. "I've been here two and half years. We've iterated on it every quarter. We're looking at all this data on what's converting and making decisions for the coming quarter's marketing spend."

The Eloqua lead scoring approach assigns leads a value from A1 through D4, with A1 being the best and hottest leads. The letter score refers to data about the prospect business demographic: job title, industry, and similar information. Some job titles and some industries are more likely to become DocuSign customers than others. The number portion of the lead score refers to the prospect's level of engagement. How often have they visited the website? How many e-mails have they opened? How often have they filled out a form for a white paper or other offer?

Eisenberg refers to this approach as "traditional" or "lead scoring 1.0." This approach still forms the foundation of DocuSign's approach, but the company is also working with suppliers, such as Lattice Engines and Mintigo, two lead-modeling software platforms that use big data to help identify the leads most likely to convert. These predictive lead scoring services analyze hundreds of data points in a company's current customer base. What industries are the companies in? What is their financial health? How active are they on social media? Have they received venture capital funding? Have they recently rented new office space?

Eisenberg said her initial reaction to Lattice Engines and Mintigo—because of DocuSign's data-based lead scoring success—was to be dismissive. But it didn't take long for her to be convinced of the potential power of these predictive lead-modeling engines. "I realized Lattice Engines does a much better job of lead scoring, because they do a regression analysis at a much bigger level. I was intrigued. As a team we were curious what it could tell us, like, Does demo convert better than trial? Lattice Engines is looking at many more attributes, and they look at all of your data and they look at a true regression analysis on what fields actually correlate to closed/won."

She adds, "This whole idea of big data comes into play. They're looking at financial databases, some of which had a derogatory mark on their data—they're not going to convert as well. Or if they've recently filed for bankruptcy, they're probably not going to buy from you."

Using big data to determine predictive lead scoring has returned some insight into DocuSign's customers. "We found through Lattice Engines that a company engaging in moderate hiring—not high or low, but moderate hiring—converts better for us."

The data also showed that companies with a certain number of pages on their websites were more likely to close, and the same with companies that tweeted 10 or more times per day. Additionally, companies that had installed a marketing automation system such as Marketo or Eloqua were also more likely to specify DocuSign. However, venture capital–backed businesses were less likely to buy the DocuSign solution. "You would think, 'They're hip, they're growing'; but they're so focused on their business they're not spending a lot of money buying other technologies necessarily," Eisenberg said.

For DocuSign, the results of predictive lead scoring have been more than interesting; they've been very positive. "We're now just in the early stages," Eisenberg said. "We only added it a few months ago, and we see a 1.1 percent increase in conversion rate. If you do about 10,000 leads a month and you have an average deal size of $6,000, over a year that equates to $6.5 million."

Real money.

How Bizo Used Data to Boost Marketing–Sales Alignment

At Bizo, which was acquired by LinkedIn in 2014 for $175 million, we are a data-driven business; our product is built on data. We have data on 120 million businesspeople. We know a person's job title, industry, size of the company the person works for, and other data. (The data is all non–personally identifiable information [non-PII].) With this anonymous data, we help marketers target and nurture audiences via display and social media advertising.

Inside Bizo, we recognize the value of data, and we have used our own data and tools to build our own business. We call it "drinking our own champagne." We have used Bizo products to target our own display and social advertising, to expand our nurturing programs beyond the e-mail inbox to incorporate display, and to personalize messages to prospects on our website.

Bizo CMO David Karel (who is now head of B2B marketing at LinkedIn) is a data-driven marketer. When he joined the company in 2010, he was the first hire in the marketing department. His first major step was beginning to build out our marketing technology stack, a process he believed was essential to creating a marketing organization that could support the sales staff in driving revenue.

Karel described his philosophy: "I was the first full-time marketing guy hired to build out the marketing engine to scale our sales effort. To leverage the small budget I had at my disposal and scale the productivity I could get out of the initial hires I would soon make, the first thing we did was to implement a marketing automation system. There was some internal debate at the time whether that investment was premature, since our programs were small scale and relatively easy to manage. That said, to conquer the very ambitious goals ahead of us, I felt it key to build scale into our marketing effort from the get-go."

Today, Bizo's marketing stack includes a marketing automation system (Eloqua), a CRM system (Salesforce.com), a content management system (SquareSpace), and many other software elements. With our reliance on data-driven marketing, Bizo has increased its marketing-sourced new revenue by more than a factor of three every year since 2010. In some key segments, marketing accounts for as much as 50 percent of Bizo's new business.

Our commitment to data-driven marketing and to marketing automation in particular is a key factor in our success. But marketing automation software is not a set-it-and-forget-it kind of system.

It requires constant monitoring and constant interpreting of the data it provides to ensure that the system of nurturing leads for the sales staff is completely optimized. And in the second quarter of 2013, the lead-generating system at Bizo took a sudden downward turn.

In the first quarter of that year, things appeared to be humming along with marketing generating 59 new sales. In the second quarter, however, that number plummeted to 26.

Bizo was growing quickly at the time. In fact, the number of account executives (AEs) on our sales team had doubled between 2012 and 2013. These new AEs needed leads, and the marketing team was determined to provide them. "The sales team was pushing hard to get those new reps productive fast," said Karel, who added, "but it's hard to scale everything at once."

Amanda Halle, who is now senior manager-marketing at LinkedIn but was previously Bizo's director of online marketing programs, described the situation this way: "Marketing found it difficult to generate sufficient lead volume to keep up with demand. To get more MQLs [marketing qualified leads] out to the sales team, the definition of an MQL began shifting almost daily in order to get enough leads out to new reps. Not surprisingly, the quality of MQLs began to decline, and new sales reps and the new sales managers grew skeptical of following up on the leads they were getting. The marketing-sourced pipeline was stagnating, and reps were not methodically following up on marketing-sourced leads. Good leads were falling off a cliff, while lower-quality leads were eating up sales productivity."

"Month over month, we saw the MQL opportunities going off the rails—way off the rails," Karel said, adding: "These were literally my darkest days at the company. We had a lot of self-doubt. I was wondering, 'Am I going to be able to solve this?'"

On the positive side, because Bizo relied on dashboards that reported trends on a weekly basis, the drop-off in lead performance was identified quickly. On the negative side, the drop-off was steep: close rates had fallen from about 15 percent to below 5 percent.

The question was how to fix the lead-generation system. Leads had a myriad of attributes, ranging from metrics that measured how engaged prospects were, to their job titles, industries, and company sizes.

"Qualifying leads is very subjective," Karel said. "It's hard to get real-time feedback from people whether the leads are good or not. So as we tried to play with our lead scoring, we were inclined to be aggressive, and we basically lowered the lead scoring threshold. We opened the gates, and we started to flood the sales team with lower-quality leads. The good leads they were also getting were getting lost or not getting much attention. The sales team—honestly, their enthusiasm was wavering pretty badly."

To solve the problem, Karel looked at the data, which indicated that a big factor in closing sales was the size of the prospect's company. Larger companies, which could handle Bizo's $10,000 per month minimum order size, closed at a far higher rate than smaller companies. In consultation with upper management and the sales chiefs, it was decided that prospects with 50 or more employees would be a minimum threshold for MQLs. Prospects that worked for companies with fewer than 50 employees would be placed in Bizo's nurturing program for its self-service program.

Once this approach was agreed upon, the marketing team began figuring out a way to add this data to the records of current and future prospects in Bizo's database. Halle described the process: "The big challenge was that we didn't have company size information for 99 percent of our leads that we had captured in our database. We immediately added company size to our forms, but it was clear that we needed to accelerate the data append effort. We ultimately used ZoomInfo to append company size to as many records as possible. In less than three weeks, we had company size appended to about 70 percent of the records in Eloqua."

In addition to pursuing a data-driven solution to this sales-marketing disconnect, Bizo also added a human element: a small sales development representative (SDR) team, managed by marketing. Via e-mail and phone, these SDRs further qualified the leads to ensure that the AEs were receiving the most highly qualified prospects possible.

Positive feedback was almost immediate. The close rate climbed again to about 15 percent. Marketing-sourced pipelines increased by 50 percent. And marketing-sourced deals saw an almost 30 percent boost. In the fourth quarter, Bizo as a whole posted a record performance.

Dan Gonzalez, formerly a sales manager at Bizo who is now sales manager, marketing solutions at LinkedIn, said, "In theory, marketing and sales are lock and key. In practice, a seasoned sales rep sometimes casts a weary eye at supposedly qualified leads. When we revamped our lead scoring and management from the ground up, I was skeptical yet cautiously optimistic. I'm proud to say our sales and marketing team took a methodical, data-centric approach, allowing our most qualified leads to receive faster, better service."

And those are lines that you'd never hear coming from the mouths of the actors in *Glengarry Glen Ross*.

CHAPTER 6

Data and the Rise of Online Advertising

Worldwide spending on programmatic online display advertising will total more than $32 billion by 2017, according to a Magna Global forecast. As that figure shows, the display advertising format has grown immensely since its quiet debut when the first Internet banner ads ran two decades ago in 1994, according to *Advertising Age*.

These ads, which included banners from AT&T and Volvo, ran on Hotwired.com, the online version of *Wired* magazine. In his *Ad Age* column from 2009, "Happy Birthday, Digital Advertising," Frank D'Angelo reflected on the 15th anniversary of the banner ad. He said that the advertising agency he was working for in 1994—Messner Vetere Berger McNamee Schmetterer (MVBMS)/Euro RSCG—embarked on the project for some of its clients as an experiment. "Let's explore the new medium and see what happens" is how D'Angelo described MVBMS's approach.

In fact, the web was so new a medium that MVBMS didn't even inform its clients of its banner ad plans. MVBMS ran into some surprises along the way. The biggest was that the ads could double as a link that would bring customers to the advertiser's website. This unexpected revelation required creating websites for some clients that didn't have them yet.

The ads were primitive. Volvo's included just the company logo and a photo of a car. The AT&T ad had a prescient and now famous call to action: "Have you ever clicked your mouse right HERE? You will." According to D'Angelo, one of the very first banner ads had a click-through rate of 78 percent, compared to today's average of less than one click in every thousand views.

These early uses of online advertising were, despite the capability to click through, really just digital versions of offline ads. What targeting existed was the same as that deployed in print or on TV: the site's demographics matched the target audience. In those early years, there was none of what was to follow online—in particular the capability to use data to target audiences anywhere they went online.

Despite that step forward, banners offered very few improvements over print advertising in those early days of the web. In fact, most banner ads were free and were value-added afterthoughts that ad sales representatives gave away on top of print advertising schedules. Formulating ad schedules was still a time-consuming and tedious process, arranged with each website individually, just as it was offline with individual print publications. And the ads were reaching business-to-business (B2B) audiences the same way as they were in vertical trade publications—based solely on the content on the site.

Early Uses of Audience Data

Although Internet advertising wouldn't achieve wide popularity for a few more years, even from its earliest days the world of advertising relied on audience data.

The first publishers of B2B trade magazines understood this reliance on data at a fundamental level. Meeting the challenge of reaching highly specific audiences, these business publishers worked on the theory that if they published content on, say, engineering, the publication would then be read by engineers. A real-life example of this concept is *Machine Design*, a publication that launched in 1929. The publication offers a subscription free of charge to many design engineers. In return, the audience receiving the free publication provides information such as their names, job titles, mailing addresses, companies, the kinds of products they design, and industries they serve.

By designing publications that catered to a specific audience, these publishers reasoned that advertisers that had products to promote would place ads to reach those audiences. B2B advertisers and their advertising agencies saw the soundness in this approach—but they wanted proof that their ads placed in *Machine Design* and other trade magazines were, indeed, reaching design engineers or whatever business audience they were targeting. They wanted proof that the magazines were being delivered, that engineers were reading the magazines, and, most important of all, that engineers were paying attention to the ads. An industry eventually grew around this distrust and the B2B advertisers' hunger for data about trade magazine readership.

Early Marketing Analytics—Audience Auditing

From the early days of scaled advertising, marketers were trying to solve the fundamental advertising question: is this ad reaching the right audience? In the early years of the twentieth century, a number of auditing organizations, such as the Alliance for Audited Media and BPA Worldwide, were founded to provide the proof needed by advertisers that their ads in magazines and newspapers were reaching the right audiences.

Of course, the industry surrounding audience verification and measurement was not limited to print. In 1950, A.C. Nielsen, now known as the Nielsen Company, began to measure TV audiences. Similarly, Arbitron estimates radio listenership. Nielsen and Arbitron sell data to advertisers and media-buying agencies; the data estimates the demographics—such as gender, age group, and income—of viewers of specific TV shows and listeners to specific radio stations.

Marketers also began to gather data that measured the performance of their ads in analog media in a variety of ways. Some trade publications included service cards, also known as bingo cards. Readers filled out the cards, indicating which ads in the magazine had interested them, and mailed the cards to the publication, which then passed the leads to the advertisers. From there, advertisers might contact the lead, send brochures of other sales material, or (as all too often happened) ignore the bingo cards because the leads were six weeks old.

While measures like the bingo cards and others that measured audiences and tracked engagement were rudimentary, they worked when collected and utilized properly. But the real breakthrough in ability to understand what consumers wanted and what was happening with marketing dollars at a fundamental level was still to come. It began with an ugly monochrome Microsoft Windows graphical browser called Mosaic that started the exponential growth of the Internet.

The Rise of Internet Advertising

When the Mosaic web browser debuted in 1993, it made the World Wide Web accessible to almost anyone. For marketers, the allure of advertising via the new browser went beyond the demographic targeting offered by print, television, and radio. The Internet promised one-to-one communications between advertisers and their targets, two-way interactivity with prospects, and virtually instantaneous feedback on ad performance—because the web enabled users to "click through" on the banners that interested them.

Of course, all of those promises are yet to be completely realized, but in the two decades of Internet advertising, marketers have moved closer to this ideal—at least in regard to one-to-one communications and interactive relationships with customers.

But it was this last promise—the ability to click through—that immediately captured the imagination of advertisers. It was after the release of Mosaic that online display advertising developed dominance, and forward-thinking marketers such as Volvo and AT&T began to realize the possibilities of these banner ads. For B2B advertisers, the click through was a digital version of the old print magazine bingo card, except the click through would improve upon that analog card by providing immediate feedback of ad performance and by allowing marketers to respond quickly to leads.

But the click through turned out not to be advertising's measurement savior, because it was just a limited proxy for the advertiser's ultimate goal of acquiring customers. Once the novelty of clicking ads to reach company websites wore off for Internet users, click-through rates (CTRs) quickly decreased to levels close to zero: only about one ad in every thousand served gets a click. True measurement of ad performance once again became complex, because low click-through rates don't mean that online advertising isn't highly effective—they just mean that CTR isn't a good metric to measure the efficacy of a message. Just like an advertiser wouldn't measure the success of a billboard at the airport by how many times someone immediately called to buy, other metrics like brand lift, boosts in website traffic, and increases in form conversions are often infinitely better gauges of online ad performance. Marketers, online publishers, and a growing group of ad technology companies began to work toward making Internet advertising more effective.

Ad Networks

The first big advance that online advertising offered to marketers beyond the simple online ad was the advertising network. As entrepreneurs realized that publisher sales teams couldn't possibly fill every ad available on their sites, they began to string together groups of sites and sell the ads as a bundle on a network. With online ad networks, marketers could contract with a single network and reach their target audience on a variety of sites across the web—as long as the sites were in the network. This arrangement appealed to publishers, because it allowed them to sell remnant inventory without adding salespeople. It appealed to marketers, because ad networks streamlined the buying process, giving marketers more reach. It also often gave them significant price reductions. Ad networks were especially beneficial for horizontal marketers—such as mobile phone plan providers, PC manufacturers, database software companies, or facilities maintenance products—that could sell their products in virtually every industry.

Audience Platforms

Another key advancement that involved the use of data in advertising was the introduction of audience platforms, which enabled marketers to target their ads to specific audiences. Ad networks still targeted via the "what"—as in what content was on the sites in the network. Audience platforms were different; these platforms targeted via the "who"—as in who were being served the ads.

Audience platforms primarily use anonymous or *non–personally identifiable information* (non-PII) contained in an Internet user's cookie to serve targeted ads no matter where that user travels on the web. The data contained in a cookie can identify, for instance, an Internet user's income level, geolocation, gender, and other attributes. B2B audience-targeting platforms are built around profiles that contain data such as the industry a businessperson works in, the size of the company, and the person's job title, job function, and seniority.

Online Advertising Exchanges

The development of online advertising exchanges was the next advancement in online display advertising, and this advancement is the one that has truly transformed Internet advertising. These exchanges, such as Google's AdX, AppNexus, and OpenX, aggregate massive scale never before attainable.

Just like the networks, the online ad exchanges are a method for publishers to sell advertising inventory to marketers. The ad exchanges have exponentially increased the usage of data in advertising on the web, and these exchanges have also boosted the effectiveness of Internet advertising. Ad exchanges offer virtually instantaneous buying and selling of online advertising in the same way that stock exchanges enable the buying and selling of shares of publicly traded companies.

A large part of the reason that data has become so important and valuable is because of the way real-time bidding (RTB) changes how ads are bought and sold. In the past, ads were sold by teams of salespeople for a fixed price. RTB is an auction where multiple bidders automatically decide how much they want to spend on an ad and bid for it—just like a computerized 20-millisecond Christie's art auction. In an art auction, different bidders will have different reasons for valuing a piece of art and varying degrees of information about what the art is worth, and the same concept applies with RTB. If 10 bidders come together to bid on an ad being served in front of a user, they may each have completely different reasons for wanting that ad to be served, and bid on the impression differently. Those reasons are entirely powered by data. One bidder might know that a person is in the market for a car from data purchased from Polk. A second bidder might know that this is a current client who recently searched for a specific product on the bidder's site. Each bidder is using data to make the split-second decision whether to bid and, if so, how much to bid. Multiply this times billions of auctions each day, and the scale of the data required to deliver a targeted, personalized, and relevant ad becomes clear.

Retargeted Display Ads

Part of the wonder of shopping on Amazon.com is that it always seems to know what you might like and thus delivers an unrivaled customer experience online. Amazon has built what is arguably the most sophisticated customer data platform and predictive modeling engine in the world. With a combination of customer search and purchase history, and predictions based on what others who have bought certain products are now buying, Amazon has been delivering a personal web, targeted e-mail, and ad experience for years. And customers have flocked to this great experience, driving exponential revenue growth of more than eight times in the past seven years.

Retargeting is a powerful and effective form of display advertising that relies on data to create a buyer experience much like the Amazon experience. Here's how it works. When an Internet user visits a company website, that company can automatically place a small bit of code, called a retargeting pixel, on that visitor's computer. The retargeting pixel enables the marketer to serve display ads to that Internet user no matter where the person travels on the Internet. The ads can have tailored messages based on the Internet user's data—that is, what website page or pages he or she visited. If a visitor only landed on the home page and then left, an ad with a branding message might be in order. If the user was browsing a specific product page and demonstrating intent to buy, an ad with a product discount or a free trial might be appropriate.

Because of the data companies have on these website visitors, retargeted ad messages can be very precise and highly effective. Retargeted ads on Facebook through the Facebook Exchange (FBX) have proved remarkably efficient, delivering low-cost and strong results.

New products hitting the market are taking retargeting and client personalization to new levels by offering sequential and dynamic ad delivery, synchronized completely with the e-mail engines like the marketing automation systems and content management systems. This end-to-end integration delivers a customer experience catered to who they are and what they care about. This smart retargeting combined with marketing automation brings the Amazon-like marketing machine to every company in the world.

Social Media Advertising's Powerful Leap Forward

Social media advertising will reach $11 billion in the United States by 2017, essentially doubling the total in 2013, according to forecasts from BIA/Kelsey and Mintel. Forty-seven percent of marketers plan to boost spending on social media, and 46 percent say they plan to maintain their spending in the next year, according to a 2013 survey by Advertising Perceptions. Marketers are spending money on this format for a simple reason: it works.

Advertising purchased through social networks such as LinkedIn and Facebook build on the advances of ad exchanges with one key improvement: LinkedIn, Facebook, Twitter, and other social networks have direct (or first-party) registration data provided by their users. This kind of information is the gold standard when it comes to online data. With this data, marketers can target their ads precisely based on job title, industry, company size, geolocation, and interests. Ads can also be targeted based on user behavior.

The financial performance of the big three social networks indicates that social media advertising continues to grow in popularity. Facebook's revenue in the second quarter of 2014 increased to $2.9 billion, up 61 percent over the second quarter of 2013. In the same time frame, LinkedIn's revenue surged 61 percent to $534 million. And Twitter more than doubled its revenue to $312 million.

How Marketers Are Putting Data on Display

Zend Technologies

At Zend Technologies, which makes tools to help streamline the software development process, Sam Adler, the company's senior director of demand generation, uses many forms of data-driven display advertising. In particular, he uses a combination of targeted display and sophisticated retargeting that nurtures prospects just like e-mail does.

In what he terms reach advertising, Adler targets information technology managers, which are Zend's primary customers for its enterprise-level product. Zend uses ad technology companies, such as Bizo, which was recently acquired in August 2014 by LinkedIn for $175 million, to identify IT managers and serve targeted display ads virtually wherever they travel on the Internet. The initial performance of this advertising has been strong, Adler said, with a cost per action (e.g., a website form fill or a purchase in the Zend Store) of around $15, and a CPC of around $11.

Adler also uses Bizo Multi-Channel Nurturing (BMN) to continue conversations with prospects who have visited the Zend corporate website. BMN enables marketers to nurture prospects by serving them targeted and sequenced display and social ads based on what portion of the website they visited and their job title, size of company they work for, industry, or other business demographics which are contained in their cookie.

BMN is designed to expand nurturing beyond the e-mail inbox. Nurturing via e-mail, while effective, has drawbacks, because fewer than 5 percent of website visitors typically subscribe to a company's e-mails. And of those who do subscribe, only 20 percent of them actually open e-mails. So nurturing with display via BMN gives marketers like Adler and Zend the opportunity to nurture prospects with targeted messages via display and social advertising.

Nurturing is crucial for Zend. Once Adler gets a conversation going with a prospect, he wants to keep it going. That's why, when a prospect fills out a form to download a white paper, for instance, Zend serves a bonus thank-you page to the prospect, which presents another bonus piece of content, such as a webinar or a YouTube video. This content is gated with a short form asking a couple of prospect profiling questions that are engaging to the user. "While they're in the store, you want to keep their attention," explained Adler, who said that the thank-you pages can see conversion rates into the 60 percent to 70 percent range, when the average form conversion is usually between 10 percent to 20 percent.

Nurturing via display and social advertising also works to keep a prospect's attention and to keep the conversation going. In serving targeted and sequenced display advertising to prospects who have already visited the company website, Zend is seeing strong results, with cost per action at $8—an excellent number. "The ROI that I see is hard to beat," Adler said.

Zuora

Zuora, which makes software for automating subscription renewals, has used display to great effect, relying on data for insight on customers, for audience targeting, and for measurement of its results.

Based on analysis of its database, Zuora uncovered the insight that its key audience is C-suite and other top executives from the finance, information technology, software, and media sectors. "Choosing to move to a subscription business model is typically an executive-led decision in most enterprises," said Brian Bell, CMO of Zuora. "We needed to find a way to reach that audience."

Using these insights, Zuora targeted its executive audience with display advertising, an effort that relies on the Bizo audience platform. At the top of the funnel, the company's display ads targeted Internet users whose profiles indicated they were executives in relevant sectors. Zuora wanted to build awareness within the largest possible relevant target audience.

In the mid-funnel, the company used display and social media advertising to engage and educate users. The display and social ads promoted tools such as an e-book that highlights the challenges and opportunities in running a subscription business model. In the lower funnel, the company used retargeted display advertising to offer a free trial of its service.

The measurement data proved the effectiveness in each part of the funnel. In the top funnel, branding efforts delivered a 28 percent increase in traffic from the target audience to the company website.

Using a combination of display ads aimed at Zuora's target audience of executives in a particular industry and BMN ads nurturing visitors to Zuora's website, the company generated a remarkable 705 total conversions in just three months' time—July, August, and September of 2014. The cost per lead was $20—incredibly low for a business where a conversion can lead to contracts worth millions of dollars.

The LiveAds

A key part of display advertising's power is the ability to optimize ads or adjust them on the fly. For instance, if an ad is delivering better results on a specific kind of website, marketers can increase their bid on that website and take money away from lesser-performing sites. Or if a certain area of the country is responding better to an ad, marketers can focus their display efforts on that region.

There's also A/B testing, where marketers will test two versions of a display ad and use the one that performs better. Dynamic display advertising takes this concept of A/B testing and supercharges it by orders of magnitude. Dynamic display advertising tests thousands of ad variations so that only the strong survive. It's like digital display Darwinism.

Here's an example of how it worked for The LiveAds, an agency that specializes in dynamic display, and one of its clients, an online retailer. For this retailer, The LiveAds developed simple creative variations. In one version, there were eight potential design templates, four different ad sizes, eight headlines, 14 photos, six offers, and two calls to action. These variations were all interchangeable, so that there were ultimately 43,008 potential combinations.

As the ads ran, analytics tools determined the best performers. The combinations that performed best were used more often, while the combinations that didn't drive conversions were quickly dropped from the rotation.

The online retailer's results with dynamic ads were impressive. The dynamic ads drove a 461 percent return on investment (ROI) during the fall and holiday season of 2012 and the Easter and Mother's Day holidays of 2013 versus the 109 percent ROI delivered by static display ads. The dynamic ads also drove a 15 percent higher-order value when compared with static ads.

"Most of the focus when you talk about big data and advertising is on media and targeting and measurement," said Sam Karow of The LiveAds. "But the same data feeds that enable all of that also enables dynamic creative."

Zendesk

Zendesk is another data-driven marketing firm. The company offers cloud-based customer service and uses data to derive customer insights, to target its audience with display advertising, and to gauge marketing results.

Zendesk's global customer base consists mainly of C-suite executives and customer service managers in the technology, retail, e-commerce, education, and professional services industries. Zendesk uses display advertising and Bizo's audience platform to target executives in its key industries. "We are targeting the right people at scale at the right time," said Michelle Carranza, Zendesk's senior manager, global advertising.

With its top-funnel display ads, Zendesk's goal is to drive brand awareness. Carranza measured the impact of its display ads in website visits from the target market. While display ads were being used, website visitors from extra large and Fortune 500 companies—a key target—climbed. Overall, more than 31,000 additional website visitors were driven to the Zendesk website while display ads were running.

In the midfunnel, Zendesk display ads that pushed educational content pieces resulted in more than 1,000 white paper downloads and webinar registrations. And in the lower funnel, display ads helped drive more than 2,000 free trials, Carranza said.

She added that Zendesk doesn't rely on a last-click attribution model to determine the contribution that various digital tactics make to top-line revenue. The last-click attribution model tends to assign inordinate value to lower-funnel tactics, such as search, because that is where the last ad before a conversion gets served—hence the term "last-click."

Instead, Zendesk uses an algorithm model that is designed to assign value not only to lower-funnel tactics but also to tactics that fill the funnel in the first place, such as display. Carranza pointed to a typical example of how a Zendesk prospect moves through the company's marketing-sales funnel. In this case, the prospect was exposed to seven display ads and clicked on one before ultimately clicking on a Google search result and then converting.

A last-click model would assign the entire value of that conversion to the Google search click. But Carranza knows better and understands the role that display played in driving that prospect through the funnel.

"This was a great example of how this algorithmic attribution model works," she said.

Online advertising has come an almost unfathomably long way in the short 20 years since the first banner ad. But the next step, powered by true understanding of the customer's buying journey and the ability to model exactly where revenue comes from, is still to come.

CHAPTER 7

Using Data to Better Understand Customers and Pursue Prospects

Sergey Brin and Larry Page. Reed Hastings. Jeff Bezos. The founders of the most successful brands of the dot-com era built their companies with a data-driven customer focus as the cornerstone of their business model. "The balance of power is shifting toward consumers and away from companies. . . . The right way to respond to this if you are a company is to put the vast majority of your energy, attention, and dollars into building a great product or service and put a smaller amount into shouting about it, marketing it," Amazon founder Jeff Bezos said in a 2010 interview with Charlie Rose, according to Inc.com.

But how do you consistently build great products? For companies such as Google, Netflix, and Internet radio service Pandora, collecting and leveraging data are essential to serving customers and creating great products for them. "If you look at the mind-blowing growth of some brands over the past couple of years, they're all brands that use data in new, intelligent ways," said Brian Kardon, CMO of predictive lead scoring company Lattice Engines.

Data-driven, customer-focused companies use the data they amass as a matter of their daily business processes to understand their customers—both individually and en masse—better with every single transaction. "Once there was only radio, and now there's Pandora," Kardon said. "Pandora is intelligent. It takes in all the data about what you like and don't like. Pandora knows what you're playing, what you like to listen to. It even knows where you're located. . . . All of these new things are replacing old things, because they have a lot more data, a lot more intelligence, and they are so much more valuable to the consumer."

Pandora is becoming increasingly popular with consumers. Pandora said it logged 1.7 billion listener hours in April 2014, which was a 30 percent increase over April 2013. Pandora is even more popular with advertisers, posting $194.3 million in revenue in the first quarter of 2014, a gain of 69 percent over the first quarter of 2013, according to a company Securities and Exchange Commission (SEC) filing.

In its original incarnation, Google operated solely as a search engine. The company used data—what the consumer typed into the search box—to provide consumers with the information they were looking for, and organized the information based on what related pages were linked to most often. These details reveal consumers' wants and needs, and Google is then able to monetize this consumer data by allowing marketers to bid on ads directed at the consumer via its AdWords platform.

With its acquisitions of YouTube in 2006 and DoubleClick in 2007, Google moved into new areas that serve marketers. Recently, Google has been expanding into new customer-focused technologies that will provide marketers with more data on consumers. Key among these acquisitions is that of Nest, a manufacturer of intelligent thermostats, in early 2014. "It's a thermostat, but it knows the outside temperature, too," Kardon said. "It knows that you like it cooler at night, but hotter during the day."

The Nest acquisition is one of Google's first moves in positioning itself for the next iteration of big data: the rise of the Internet of Things, in which a variety of electrical and electronic products, ranging from refrigerators to jet engines, send signals about customer usage back to manufacturers, distributors, and retailers.

Netflix Flexes Its Data Muscle

Netflix, at first glance, doesn't seem to be a data-driven business. In its infancy, the video rental company's chief differentiator was an innovative delivery approach, one that saved consumers a dreaded trip to the video store and eliminated exorbitant late fees by shipping movie and TV series DVDs via the U.S. Postal Service. This unlikely and counterintuitive innovation, almost on its own, sent Blockbuster and its ilk into bankruptcy.

But data has always been a part of Netflix's approach. With its subscribers providing their viewing preferences in their queue—not to mention the movies and TV shows they actually watched and when and how often they watched them—Netflix gained deep insight into its customers' viewing habits. The company also knows where its customers live. And now, with the advent of streaming, Netflix knows even more about its customers and their viewing habits than ever. The company, for example, knows when viewers pause, rewind, or fast-forward what they're watching.

One of the ways Netflix is leveraging this data first became crystal clear when the company funded and developed its own TV series, *House of Cards*, which debuted in 2013. Netflix executives took the unusually aggressive move of putting up $100 million to green-light two full 13-episode seasons of the show.

The reason they felt so confident? Big data.

When they were pitched the show, which other content producers took a pass on, Netflix executives consulted the data they had on the viewing habits of the company's almost 30 million subscribers, according to David Carr's *New York Times* article, "Giving Viewers What They Want," published February 24, 2013. Netflix executives confirmed that their subscribers watched David Fincher–directed movies such as *The Social Network*. They also watched movies starring Kevin Spacey. And many had downloaded the original British version of *House of Cards*. Netflix could even tailor its marketing of the show, serving Spacey-themed trailers to its users who had watched his films, Fincher-themed trailers to *The Social Network* fans, and a differently edited trailer to users who had seen the original *House of Cards*. As Carr wrote in his article, "With those three circles of interest, Netflix was able to find a Venn diagram intersection that suggested that buying the series would be a very good bet on original programming."

That big data–inspired bet was indeed a very good one, as the binge viewing of the *House of Cards* series by Netflix subscribers will attest.

Amazon is also moving into content creation, in both publishing and video production. Like Netflix, Amazon's beginnings were simply delivery of goods. Amazon started as an online bookseller and quickly moved into selling other entertainment, such as music and movies. Its recommendation engine—an algorithm that suggests books, CDs, or DVDs a user might be interested in based on what similar users had already bought—is uncannily accurate and wildly successful.

Amazon long ago moved beyond selling entertainment to selling virtually any consumer goods, ranging from electronics to patio furniture. The company has even moved into selling industrial products, a move that has brought it into competition with industrial distributors such as Grainger and McMaster-Carr. Today, Amazon is one of the most effective e-commerce engines ever invented.

In addition to convenience and ease of use, data underpins Amazon's success. Each new purchase by a user only makes Amazon's recommendation engine that much more accurate.

"Of course," Brian Kardon said, "Amazon is the king. It knows what you put in your shopping cart—what you covet but didn't buy. It knows your product ratings, where you live, what your neighbors buy. If you live in Chicago, Amazon doesn't have to know it's snowing, but they know that your neighbor just bought a shovel and eight pounds of salt."

That's incredibly valuable real-time marketing information, and constantly collecting and using data like that to deliver offerings its customers want is central to Amazon's business model.

SaaS and Its Powerful Window on the Customer

Big data and its insight into customers isn't reserved for dot-com giants such as Amazon, Netflix, and Google. Other relatively new business models also have customer data at their core. The software as a service (SaaS) business model, where software is hosted and managed on shared servers instead of installed at a customer site, is a prime example. Joe Payne, former CEO of Eloqua, a marketing automation software company that deploys a SaaS model, said SaaS provides powerful advantages via its insight into customers. Payne left the company after taking it public and its $957 million sale to Oracle, a deal that closed in 2013.

"I think what's interesting about the technology phase we are in today is that for the first time we have a pretty good sense of how people are using our software and when they're using, how frequently they're using, and how many people are using it," Payne said. "If you pay attention to all those things, it can give you insight that will help you win your market."

Among other things, the software gives marketers the capability to know how many users are logging in on a daily basis. Payne said SaaS companies can take advantage of this data to gain insights into the products, to help customers, and maybe to even set them straight on occasion.

"We had all of our customers' history month by month in our system," Payne said, ". . . and when a client would call in for support or with a complaint, sometimes they might call and say, 'We don't use the system and it's not working for us.' And we'd say, 'Wait a minute, let's go back and look at your monthly totals, how many contacts you have under management, how many e-mails you send, how many programs you're running,' and they would be like, 'Wow, I didn't know that.'

"They wouldn't know their own usage in the system and we would know the usage. We could help them understand just how much they were using product."

Payne also said that a SaaS software company's window into product usage is a view that can help in future product development. "If everybody seems to be using a certain area of the product," he said, "there might be opportunity to expand that area. If everybody is not using a certain area, there might be an opportunity to deprecate that functionality, which in software land never happens."

The Power of Predictive Lead Modeling

Other companies are getting into the act by providing platforms to generate insights for their clients. Companies such as Lattice Engines, FlipTop, 6Sense, and other similar predictive lead modeling companies use big data to create algorithms that help their marketer clients with predictive lead scoring. Essentially, these companies analyze a marketer's current client base—or a segment of its clients—to determine what characteristics make a good customer; then the marketers go seek out other candidates with the same attributes. The algorithms are complex and bring together both online and offline data, and go far beyond what marketers would pay attention to in the past, but the point is that this data can yield valuable insights.

"The big challenge for marketers is that the data resides in different silos," Lattice Engines' CMO Brian Kardon said. "We append thousands of additional pieces of information onto a marketer's customer data, like what technologies their customers use, are they hiring people, their international presence, are they posting jobs, what kind of jobs, how many titles they have, what are they doing in social, what is their credit rating. So, we look at all these additional attributes, and we can actually tell your company which of all your prospects are most likely to buy. We apply predictive models on all your data, we supplement it with additional external data, and we're able to tell you who is most likely to buy and why."

Facts like "are they hiring people" seem like they are outside of the scope of what a marketer would need to know. But big data shows correlation with positive conversion rates, and this is the whole point. Big data is exposing historically hidden understanding. The data is hiding in plain sight, and marketers need to leverage everything that is discoverable about a potential customer.

One of Lattice's customers is Autodesk, a maker of computer-aided design/computer-aided manufacturing (CAD/CAM) software for design engineers. Lattice analyzed the characteristics of Autodesk's customers and found a striking attribute that is associated with buying from Autodesk: is this company hiring design engineers and is the phrase "CAD/CAM" in the job description? Companies with this characteristic were many times more likely to buy CAD/CAM software within 90 days.

Another Lattice customer is Juniper Networks, a manufacturer of Internet switches and routers. Lattice analyzed Juniper's sales looking for common threads among hundreds of attributes. "We looked at about 800 attributes, and the one attribute that mattered the most was whether someone had signed a new lease to move offices in the last 90 days," Kardon said. "Someone who signed a new lease is three times more likely to want to buy switches or routers than someone who isn't. When you move to a new office you want more technology backbone."

So Juniper added this additional criterion into how it determines potential prospects. "Our crawlers harvest information from more than 150 million websites each day, including all sorts of real estate records, municipal records, government records, and legal records, and we find people who sign leases," Kardon said. "We immediately forward that to a salesperson, and the salesperson is notified in their CRM system, 'Call the prospect right now because they just signed the lease and congratulate them on moving to a new office.'"

Another Lattice customer, office supply retailer Staples, found that companies hiring new employees were also more likely to buy more office supplies. "Three years ago, they would call and say, 'What do you need this week from Staples?' and the customer would say, 'Well, I don't know,'" Kardon said. "Now they call and say, 'Congratulations, you hired five new people, and you're going to need more desks and chairs, and probably you're going to need another printer, because your old printer can cover only six work stations.'"

Data Isn't Reserved for Dot-Coms

Lattice Engines, FlipTop, and 6Sense aren't the only companies leveraging big data principles to help marketers. Merit Direct, a company that manages direct-mail lists for publishers and marketers, offers similar analysis to its customers. One customer is Edmund Optics, a business-to-business (B2B) catalog and e-commerce company that sells lenses, cameras, lasers, and other optics products.

Marisa Edmund is executive vice president of marketing and communications at Edmund Optics, a company that doesn't have a

CRM system and is in the process of rolling out more robust enterprise resource planning software. So Edmund—both the company and the marketing executive—uses the services and data Merit Direct offers to help manage its global database of 240,000 customers and prospects. Merit uses big data to help Edmund identify the attributes of its best customers. Using this data, Edmund can seek out potential prospects with similar characteristics via the postal mail and via e-mail.

"We can use a predictive model to analyze new customers on any given day," Edmund said. "And with the model that Merit Direct built, we can identify the top 10 percent that should be good customers, that should be volume customers based on looking at our current big customers."

Merit Direct's predictive modeling looks at thousands of characteristics, and typically about 25 to 50 of those attributes are statistically important to determining whether a company may be a good prospect for Edmund Optics, Marisa Edmund said. In practice, Merit can help Edmund Optics by examining its new customers and identifying those most likely to become huge buyers.

"Then I can go and specifically target those promising prospects," Edmund said. "I can send them an automated welcome kit. My printer will do it for me where they put together a variable printing piece that says, 'Dear New Customer, I saw you were interested in buying prisms; here's a six-page handout about prisms; welcome to the Edmund's family; thanks so much.'"

Edmund Optics can also segment customers who are buying a specific product line and then use big data to target other customers who have similar characteristics and perhaps should also be buying that product line. "Merit can look at customers who are already buying this product line and say, out of all my customers, if they are not buying this product line now, who should be buying this product line?" Edmund said. "And then they gave me a list of 1,600 accounts that should be buying this product line but they aren't."

Edmund Optics was founded more than 70 years ago. You don't have to be a dot-com to use big data to glean valuable information from your customer base. Every company, no matter how old or how new, no matter whether it is in an ancient industry or in high tech, will need to make use of data if it wants to thrive.

CHAPTER 8

The Arrival of Left-Brained Leaders and the Rise of the Marketing Department

Traditionally, creative people who have found themselves working in business have gravitated toward careers in marketing and advertising. At advertising agencies, there's even a place of honor for this sort of people: the creative department.

In the television show *Mad Men* that portrays a 1960s-era advertising agency, the protagonist has many characteristics of a right-brained person. Don Draper is a creative type with a penchant for developing ad concepts that bail him and his agency brethren out at the last minute. There's precious little data informing Draper's campaigns. What he delivers to clients is all about the ineffable, immeasurable power of creative ideas.

The very first episode of *Mad Men* showcases Draper's approach to his work as he struggles to come up with an advertising concept for Lucky Strike cigarettes. He jots ideas on a cocktail napkin in a bar. He throws a research report in the trash. And finally, at the crucial meeting, as he stalls for time asking the owners of Lucky Strike how their cigarettes are made, the idea hits him in a flash of insight: "It's toasted."

What's interesting about Draper's creativity and his persuasiveness is that the goal is first and foremost about selling the client on the idea. Actually selling cigarettes to consumers is secondary.

But by the seventh season of *Mad Men*, a computer—not a PC but a boxy IBM System/360 mainframe—is installed in the Sterling Cooper & Partners agency. The mainframe makes some people, Draper included, nervous, perhaps because it will have the power to determine whether their advertising campaigns are actually working.

In fact, one character, Michael Ginsberg, becomes unhinged upon the computer's arrival. "What am I, Cassandra?" he says. "That machine came for us, and one by one . . ."

The trajectory of the advertising industry that is depicted in the *Mad Men* series over its first seven seasons has a lot of similarities to the changes that are now gripping the marketing world. Data and the brain are triumphing over raw creativity and gut feelings. Technology is inexorably barging into the marketing department.

And despite the discomfort that the *Mad Men* characters display regarding computers, the end result of data's increasing role in marketing has led to the department's rise in business importance.

As data-driven digital marketing has become the predominant model of marketing, the kinds of people who practice marketing and advertising are certainly different sorts than they used to be even five years ago, let alone in the *Mad Men* era. There are more mathematically inclined people in marketing now—and a diminishing number of would-be novelists and screenwriters.

"The vast majority of CMOs out there—maybe really the entire marketing department—are what we call right-brained people," said Glenn Gow, CEO of Crimson Marketing. "They are hired for their creative abilities and their ability to drive outbound marketing campaigns and then do branding. The world has changed very, very quickly, and it requires left-brain talent. It requires people who can make sense of the data that's coming in."

In the past, a major responsibility of the CMO was managing the relationship between the company and the ad agency and finding the creative genius who could deliver blockbuster TV spots and memorable slogans. "Diamonds are forever." "Just do it." "Where's the beef?" And, of course, "It's toasted."

Joe Hix is representative of the statistically and mathematically oriented people who are increasingly participating in the marketing and advertising world. He grew up in a household with a left-brained bent. He says his mother, Janet Soldan, was a statistician for the National Collegiate Athletic Association (NCAA) and used a data-driven approach to become an ace fantasy football player. Hix said he learned to use Excel spreadsheets before he learned to use a calculator. At the University of Oklahoma he had a triple major in computer science, business administration, and marketing.

After graduating in 2003, he put those disciplines to work at a small, Dallas-based agency called New Media Gateway, which was a pioneer in helping marketers create 360-degree views of their customers across interactions in search, e-mail, and even offline channels. At New Media Gateway, Hix began to see the value of a data-driven, customer-focused approach.

"We recognized that it wasn't about customizing channels; it was about customizing experiences across all channels," Hix said, adding: "We were ahead of the market. We would be going and pitching this stuff, and people would look at us like, 'Are you crazy? You are going to do dynamic print that has an integrated personalized URL that's going to have integrated personalized numbers for a given offer, for a given product, for a given segment, and you are going to coordinate that with media and coordinate that with billboards?'"

It was a hard sell, Hix recalls, with many potential clients insisting that what they were proposing was simply not possible. "We were a bunch of young guys," he said. "We didn't have any gray hairs to say to us, 'No, they are right.' So we created true integrated data sets when we would actually demo this that could prove out—at a customer record level—the value of personal integration and cohesive experiences across all channels. So in our business alone we had to use big data, because we had to show our initial clients that we could make this work."

First the smaller clients hired New Media Gateway, and then the big ones did. "We went from being a nobody shop to landing AT&T, Verizon, T-Mobile, Sprint—and that is just telco," Hix said. "We had every major Internet carrier. We had every major financial institution almost overnight."

After New Media Gateway, Hix honed his data-driven, customer-focused mentality at other agencies such as Omnicom's Enterprise Spectrum, Javelin Direct, and now Moxie Interactive, where he is senior vice president of technology strategy and a key part of his role is still helping marketers develop a 360-degree view of their customers.

"The goal," he said, "is to create infrastructure and framework up and down every touch point of the enterprise and across the marketing spectrum so that, starting with acquisition all the way through churn, we are constantly adding to your profile. That starts at the very beginning with collecting true structured marketing metadata, essentially like hooks on a fishing line. We are constantly tagging that back to the metadata structure, so we know Joe was in the acquisition campaign to add a line with a smartphone in Texas last year, and he clicked on this link, which was tied to this offer."

Hix stresses that the capability to use data to know customers and prospects better is real, and he no longer—as he had to do a decade ago—must work so hard to convince marketers of the possibilities. "It is not about feasibility anymore," he said. "It is about value."

For instance, by identifying and targeting prospects with the highest potential lifetime value, marketers can use targeted offers with an eye on generating more revenue for their companies. Additionally, marketers can also spend less (or nothing) on trying to lure prospects whose lifetime value is marginal. "Marketers tell me, 'I want to raise revenue by 10 percent,'" Hix said. "I tell them, 'What if I could drop your spend by 50 percent? Is that raising the bottom line?' And they say, 'Yeah, okay. Cool.'"

This kind of positive financial impact doesn't require a huge investment, Hix says. He has helped marketers build integrated databases with open source software and inexpensive blade servers. "With big data, people think that they have to go invest billions of dollars or millions of dollars to get started. They don't. You can do it on open source almost for free," Hix said.

Well, as long as you can find the people with the combination of marketing and computer science degrees to help you build it.

Individuals like Hix who have technology backgrounds are increasingly a central part of marketing departments as they grapple with installing and implementing marketing automation software, analytics tools, and other elements of the marketing stack. "How the Presence of a Chief Marketing Technologist Impacts Marketing," a report by Gartner, a research firm that focuses on the technology sector, found that 81 percent of big companies had a chief marketing technologist or equivalent position in 2014. That figure was up from 70 percent a year earlier. (Both figures are likely higher than among nontech businesses.) Gartner defines a marketing technologist as a person whose responsibilities include "aligning marketing technology with business goals."

Nick Panayi, director of global brand and digital marketing at Computer Sciences Corporation (CSC), divides his marketing team into three kinds of people. "Content jockeys," the ones who write blogs, produce videos, and compose white papers, are the closest to the traditional creative types. The other two roles are much more math and technology oriented. The "infrajockeys" architect, run, and maintain the marketing technology ecosystem, and "demand gen jockeys" optimize demand generation efforts using sophisticated marketing automation systems.

Brian Krause is the vice president of global marketing and communications at Molex Incorporated, a top manufacturer of electronic interconnect solutions. He has worked in the industry for more than three decades and he credits his success in the last eight years to being focused on the data-driven, digitally focused approach of his team, who represent a blend of seasoned and younger professionals. "One of many things we do right at Molex is hire the best people," Krause said. "Often the best people are not only fiercely intelligent, but ask tough questions and challenge the status quo, not simply for the sake of being heard, but out of a passion to improve how we as a company connect with our customers. From a leadership perspective, that requires recognition of better ideas—and knowing when to let go—to give talented people space to collaborate and bring the best ideas to fruition. The development of our social media program is a good example, leveraging our diverse expertise across the globe to define a social media direction and build out an effective platform for reaching audiences. Molex has been engaging with customers, employees, and partners through social media for more than six years now, which is a tremendous accomplishment for a B2B company."

At some companies, especially in the technology sector, even CMOs have come up through the technical side of the business. Matt Ackley is now the CMO and senior vice president of product at Marin Software, which offers a digital advertising management platform, but he got his introduction to marketing at eBay, where he was a software programmer. "I was not a marketing person to begin with," Ackley says. "I actually used to code for a living, so I can tell people I was dragged kicking and screaming into the world of marketing. But the reason I went in to marketing is because back in 2005 eBay recognized that, one, it needed to do a better job of online marketing, and, two, it was going to be a data-driven exercise—so they wanted technical people in that organization."

Ackley says the best marketing organizations must embrace the role that people with technology backgrounds can play. "Marketing departments should have developers who can create dynamic ads, who can maybe run a test and write their own mobile app," he said. "I do think that the CMO needs to be as much a product manager as somebody with a marketing background."

The creative part of the CMO job can be developing ad concepts, but now that part of the role also includes creating new technologies that are, in and of themselves, marketing efforts. "Marin is an SEM [search engine marketing] platform," Ackley said. "It's a general marketing platform, but what is essentially Marin, I built that at eBay. We built the tool that interfaces with Google AdWords. We built the tools that interface with Microsoft's AdCenter. . . . We built our own affiliate platform [at eBay], and because we built our own platforms, we built our own bidding algorithms. So, for instance, if I wanted to do day-parting on search [bidding only on certain parts of the day], I actually built that into our application at eBay—the ability to bid different amounts for different keywords at different times of the day. We built that before Google built that."

Building this kind of technology is the new marketing creative. "When I ran marketing at eBay, I was actually more of a product manager than a CMO," Ackley said. "In a sense, we were designing technology and algorithms to acquire and retain users. I did not spend a lot of time thinking about brand messaging and creative and whatnot. If we had a creative question, we just tested it."

This data-driven approach worked. It gave eBay control, speed, and insight. "We gained an advantage over everybody else," Ackley said, "because we learned how to use our data early. We were able to do this quickly, because we had the right organizational structure. I had a development team that reported to me. I had an analytics team that reported to me, so I didn't have to run off to core eBay product management to build a search bidding tool." And now he runs marketing for Marin, a company bringing the power of what he built at eBay to other companies around the world.

At Domo, a fast-growth business intelligence software company, Heather Zynczak, who is the company's CMO, has a background that has a lot in common with Ackley's. "I started out my career in coding," she said. "I worked at Andersen Consulting back in the early 1990s, back before there was a lot of packaged software."

Zynczak got an MBA from Wharton, a metrics-oriented school. After graduation, she worked at Booz Allen Hamilton and Boston Consulting Group, where she focused on marketing with a numbers approach. Stints in product management and marketing at Oracle and SAP only sharpened her mathematics-based approach to her trade.

"I don't think of myself as a typical marketer," she said, "and I'll tell you why I feel like I'm a good marketer at this stage of the marketing evolution. If you think back to the 1960s and the marketing world back 20, 30, 40 years ago, you just had to be super-creative. You came up with an amazing idea and then you sat back enjoying martini lunches until you won an award for it later in the year. Things are wildly different today. Yes, creative is extremely important, but you can measure whether your creative is good creative within minutes. Everything is extremely data-driven, and marketing can now be accountable for ROI."

Ironically, Zynczak makes the case that this numbers-driven focus allows room for even more creativity by the marketing team. "There is this conversation going on right now among the marketing community of 'Are we getting too data-driven? And is it going to hurt our creativity?'

"I would emphatically say, 'No! It's going to help us.' I let the younger people on our team come up with new and unconventional ideas. I let them run with them, as long as they are within a certain budget. They'll try new ideas, and because we test them, in a couple of days I'm going to know. This approach has produced some of our best marketing efforts. I think we're creative, because we take those risks. It's like with my data I have a parachute. I'm okay jumping off that cliff, because I've got the data parachute behind me."

With more access to data, marketers are better able to prove that their spending leads to revenue. Instead of being a cost center, many CMOs have proven—or are on the way to proving—that their department is actually a profit center.

"Marketing is sitting on top of this treasure trove of data," Crimson's Gow said. "They are being pressured to contribute to revenue in some way, and they're trying to make sense of these two pressures: I have all the data, but I don't know what to do with it; and now I am being told I need to contribute to revenue. So we believe that there are opportunities for data scientists and marketing people and the CMO to integrate this data in a way that you can gain insight; you can do the targeting; you can do the measurement."

With data, marketers also gain clearer insight into customers and prospects, which has given them more input into their company's future direction. Changes in the buyer's journey, where prospects conduct much of their research online, have elevated marketing, because the department has a unique perspective on the company's target audience. As CSC's Panayi pointed out, marketers "all owe a debt of gratitude to the Corporate Executive Board for the research they've done around the buyer's journey turning largely digital. A lot of prospective customer-buying 'signals' are now digital and increasingly difficult for sales to identify. In sales organizations, where marketing was often seen as not that relevant, guess what: about 57 percent of the buyer's journey is now known to be digital. Sales knows full well that only marketing can shed light on that 57 percent, so this shift has increased the level of communication and interaction between sales and marketing tenfold."

With this insight that the buyer is doing the vast majority of product research before ever talking to a sales rep, marketers play a larger role in steering their company's future. A March 2014 IBM report, "Stepping Up to the Challenge: CMO Insights from the Global C-Suite Study," found that 63 percent of CMOs have "involvement in business strategy development." Among other C-suite executives (other than the CEO), only CFOs, at 72 percent, were more regular contributors to strategy. Only 42 percent of CIOs were involved in business strategy.

"We are the last to come to the table in this data revolution," Domo's Zynczak said of the marketing department, "but arguably the most important."

At some companies, former CMOs have risen to the CEO spot, a job formerly reserved for executives who came out of operations or finance. In an August 23, 2013, CMO.com article, "Why More Marketers Are Taking the CEO Reins," Thomas Yang, a partner at consultancy PrimeGenesis, named a handful of companies that had recently named former CMOs to the top job:

- Royal Dutch Shell named Ben van Beurden its CEO. He was previously the company's director of refining and marketing operations.
- RadioShack named Joseph Magnacca as CEO. He was previously CMO of Walgreen Co.
- Ruby Tuesday appointed JJ Buettgen president and CEO. He was previously CMO of Darden Restaurants.
- Audi of America named Scott Keogh, its former CMO, to the CEO role.

- Mercedes-Benz USA elevated former CMO Steve Cannon to CEO.
- Gilt Groupe named former Citigroup CMO Michelle Peluso as CEO.

Yang explained the trend: "Companies have no choice but to better understand customers' needs. It's a necessity for success—and survival. The call for more customer-centric strategies starts at the top." Restated, marketers are the closest to the voice of the customer and have the most significant ability to move shareholder value. It is only a matter of time before they are running the entire organization and instilling customer-centric cultures to drive success.

Joe Zawadzki, CEO of MediaMath, a company that describes itself as a marketing operating system, is a big believer in data's role in marketing. He says the rise of the marketing department is driven by results, metrics, and data.

"There is definitely a new class of marketer," Zawadzki said. "I think of it as outcomes-driven as opposed to inputs-driven; that is, it's about results. It's a P and L role. That's a seat at the big boy table when you tie your effort to bottom-line results directly.

"The old CMO was really focused on 'What am I spending on TV, and what am I spending on direct mail and print?' Now, it's much more about what's working. 'How do I reallocate based on ROI? And how can I just make more prudent investments that produce better results?' Because the metrics are increased and becoming the same metrics that the CEO and CFO look at."

Only by aligning their goals and metrics with the CEO's business objectives can marketing executives rise from the marginal position they have too often held within their companies. Joe Payne, former CEO of Eloqua, explains that marketers need to be more focused on business metrics than, for example, the latest modifications to an ad campaign: "I always encouraged my marketers to come to the weekly meeting with the same data every week," Payne explained. "The sales guy comes with the forecast. He doesn't come with the forecast and then the next week with some other thing. The CFO doesn't make up his own metric. He doesn't say, 'I don't like that cash flow statement that we use for GAAP, so I've made up my own cash flow statement.' . . . I think the CMO finally has the data to say, 'Here are our numbers this week. Here's where we are against our target.'"

Payne doesn't doubt that the marketing department has always been a contributor. The difference now is that marketers have the data, tools, and metrics to prove it.

"It was very hard for marketers to articulate how they were contributing," Payne said. "It's like Supreme Court Justice Potter Stewart, who said he couldn't define pornography, but 'I know it when I see it.' And that's the thing about good marketing. Most people are like, 'I can't tell you what good marketing is, but when I see it, I know it.' That's just how it was with marketing. But now we can judge marketing based on results, and the hardest part that I've found in my career in the last 10 years, or even the last five years, is to get the CMO to come to every meeting with the same report week after week."

But marketing executives at a variety of companies are putting Payne's advice into action. These marketing executives are focusing on data when they present at company meetings. The response by other C-suite executives to this approach has been quite positive.

Domo's Zynczak prides herself on being data driven and, like an increasing number of businesspeople, believes marketers must be held accountable for their spending and for producing bottom-line results. Still, too many marketers are not being held to this standard, she says. "How many marketers are held accountable for ROI?" she asked. "How many marketers are expected to know their contribution? And how many marketers are held accountable in the co-op plan for the number of leads they generate, or the engagement rate of customers, or customer satisfaction? How many marketers have started to show their own value?"

Zynczak counts herself and her team as being among the marketers who are demonstrating their value. "We're actually being held accountable on what we provide the company," she said. "What's our revenue contribution? Give me a hard number—not 'we won a marketing award.'"

When she is in a meeting with her fellow C-suite executives at Domo, marketing is on equal footing with finance, product, information technology, and other departments. "Marketing is such a big part of the company, and I am a valued member of that team," Zynczak said. "It's no longer that the finance guys, with the CEO and our president, sit down and work out the model and then just come tell marketing what my budget is and what I need to hit. Now, I take part in those discussions, because I provide value from a data perspective."

At Edmund Optics, Marisa Edmund, the company's vice president of marketing and communications, said that having access to data has given her department an elevated role in the business. "Ninety-nine percent of what we do in marketing now is based on data and analytics and has been made easier by being online," Edmund said. "For example, we recently did a presentation to our upper management leadership team. That presentation was regarding SEO [search engine optimization] and SEM [search engine marketing] and how it works. It had statistics and looked at conversions and how we track some of these online metrics. Every point we made was backed up by a number or a ROI technical statistic. Our CFO after the meeting said, 'I loved your presentation. I loved that everything had numbers, and I loved that I can trace it back and understand what you're doing based on that and see how it assists in growing the company.'"

This data-driven approach beloved by CFOs is not reserved for marketers like Edmund Optics. There is nothing special about the company that makes it predisposed to a statistically based approach to marketing. At virtually every business, marketing is in a position to excel because of metrics, because of data.

Lisa Arthur, CMO of Teradata Marketing Applications and the author of *Big Data Marketing* (John Wiley & Sons, 2013), said she fears many marketers may be blowing this opportunity to play a bigger role in their company's destiny. She continued by saying that this opportunity is guaranteed for the marketing department and the CMOs and their teams have to seize it.

"There's a worry that marketing has a history of going off and doing their own thing in the silos that we talk about in the book," Arthur said. "Marketing potentially will miss this opportunity that big data provides. What's next is we need to show we get it, and then demonstrate how to use data for differentiation and ultimately to drive value for the customer, which will drive value for the business."

Joe Payne says some CMOs and other marketing leaders will have to struggle against their own innate creative tendencies. They will need to rise above a sometimes deeply held bias against the numbers and statistics that link marketing with the overall goals of the business. Many marketers resist this directive, Payne says, because they say, "If I wanted to be boring, I would have been a CFO."

A numbers-driven approach is now not only possible but necessary to be successful. "When the executive team gets used to looking at that data," Payne says, "then they get good at identifying what the issues are and what their bottlenecks are. And then they might say, 'You're having problems getting people at the top of the funnel. What are you doing about that?' And the CMO will say, 'Let me tell you what's working and what's not working.'"

And then a dialogue begins to solve the problem in a data-driven way. And when those dialogues start happening consistently, the company is on its way to being data driven.

CHAPTER 9

Implementing a Big Data Plan (Sometimes by Thinking Small)

Big data is an intimidating concept. It sounds hard. It sounds overwhelming. It sounds expensive.

Data has always been with us. The difference now is that is it more accessible and more immediate. Data, lots of it, is available in real time.

"It's been here for a very long time," Vinny Sosa, director of web intelligence and optimization at Citrix Systems, marketers of GoToMeeting, said of big data. "Now it just has a name."

The key to getting big data right at your company is not to get bogged down with the concept of big data. Start by identifying the needs of your customers and your business. Also, think small—focus on the parts of data you think can change your business for the better, not on the entirety of the data available to you. Keep in mind the old proverb: The journey of a thousand miles begins with a single step.

Note that leveraging data is not reserved for big companies. Big companies do have advantages, such as deep pockets. But small companies have advantages, too. For instance, they are nimble and are often not tied down by legacy systems and data siloed in various corners of the company.

It's instructive to examine how George Stenitzer approached bringing more data and analytics into his marketing department when he was the vice president of communications at Tellabs back in 2010. Stenitzer focused first on what he wanted. He knew Tellabs, a telecommunications equipment company, had been investing a significant amount in its website. Not only was Tellabs investing time and money into building the website and populating it with content, but it was also investing in search engine optimization, e-mail promotion, display advertising, and other tactics to drive prospects to the site.

Stenitzer, who now runs his own marketing consulting firm, Crystal Clear Communications, didn't believe that Tellabs was getting its money's worth from its website. He wanted more "soft conversions" from site visitors; he defined soft conversions as reading a blog post, watching a video, or interacting with certain other content on the site without having to supply an e-mail address. He also, of course, wanted more "hard conversions," where prospects shared their e-mail addresses to download white papers and other similar content.

In 2010, Tellabs was generating soft conversions at about a 10 percent rate, meaning that one out of every 10 visitors to the site interacted with a piece of Tellabs content. Stenitzer wanted to improve that rate. At the same time, he wanted to demonstrate marketing's contribution to revenue. To accomplish these goals, both of which required collecting and analyzing more data, he took three basic steps:

First, he revamped Tellabs.com to encourage more content interaction.

Next, he invested in new analytics tools from IBM and marketing automation technology from marketing automation firm Marketo.

And finally, he used these software tools both to measure his content efforts and to nurture prospects in the Tellabs e-mail database toward becoming genuine leads and ultimately customers.

In revamping Tellabs.com, Stenitzer identified that four basic kinds of content were responsible for the company's soft conversions: blogs, videos, ungated white papers, and articles from Tellabs' custom publication, *Insight*.

He also sorted Tellabs' content into four tiers, based on the amount of time the content demanded of prospects. The first tier asked for no more than seven seconds of a prospect's time. This content included headlines on the Tellabs.com home page that pointed readers to other content on the site. This approach put the path to content front and center on the company website. In addition to these headlines on the website, these seven-second bursts of content also comprised tweets and Facebook and LinkedIn posts that drove prospects to Tellabs content.

The second content tier asked for two minutes of a prospect's time. This tier included blog posts and web pages, each about

400 words long, and short web videos typically about two minutes in length. The third tier asked for five minutes of time and consisted of longer videos and articles. The last tier consisted of detailed white papers that required 20 minutes or more from a prospect.

"If we can get you with that seven seconds of attention, the idea is I want to ladder you up to two minutes," Stenitzer said.

Stenitzer organized the entire website around this concept of laddering up content. "I think the main idea that we had when we rebuilt the Tellabs.com website was: how do we make the customer's path to conversion easy?" Stenitzer said. "We rewrote it from scratch, and we had in mind that what we wanted to do was get customers to go along the path with us, starting with a soft conversion."

Focusing on how to ease the customer's path to conversion, Stenitzer and his team relentlessly analyzed data delivered by the IBM analytics tool that indicated what was being read and what pathways prospects were taking—or not taking—to get there.

One pathway to enticing readers into deeper engagement was to list links to related content on the right-hand side of Tellabs.com web pages. But the data showed that prospects were not clicking on a text link to "PDF Resources." To make these PDFs more noticeable, Stenitzer placed a red button on the right-hand side that read "PDF Resources."

"Until that big red button got planted in the right column, nobody even noticed the PDF link," Stenitzer said. "One of the first things we saw with our Net Analytics from IBM was that nobody went there. We had all this great content that people were missing, and the red button helped change that."

The IBM analytics helped Tellabs determine which content was performing best. At regular meetings, members of the marketing staff would discuss what the analytics indicated. "It's like, 'This is working; let's do more of it,'" Stenitzer said. "'This isn't working; let's get rid of it.' And that's what the data tells you."

The analytics also demonstrated the value of white papers, which require at least a 20-minute commitment to read from start to finish. "If I take my top five white papers, I actually get more hits on them than on the top five videos or on the top five blogs or the top five *Insight* articles," Stenitzer said. "So, even though the white papers are long-form content, when you get a serious buyer who's going down the path toward a purchase, that white paper is really important, and they pay a lot of attention to it. While I put emphasis on the seven seconds, two minutes, five minutes, and then 20 minutes, one of the surprises that we got from the analytics is 20 minutes is where they really want to go."

But did all of this effort pay off? Stenitzer said the soft conversion data proves it did. From the time the website was revamped with a data-driven approach focused on pointing prospects to content, soft conversions increased every year. "Back in 2010, our soft conversions were running about 10 percent," Stenitzer said. "By 2011, they were 20 percent. By 2012, they were 30 percent. In 2013, they were right around 40 percent, and in 2014, they hit 46 percent."

But getting more content read by more prospects isn't worth much if it doesn't lead to more marketing-sourced revenue. So at the same time he was revamping Tellabs.com, Stenitzer was also strengthening a data-driven demand generation team that used Marketo marketing automation software.

As part of this effort, Tellabs hired a demand generation manager to optimize usage of Marketo software. Many Tellabs white papers were gated content, meaning that a prospect had to provide an e-mail address and other information in exchange for downloading the white paper. At first, Tellabs required 13 fields on the forms that prospects had to fill out to download the white paper. Data showed that five fields enticed more prospects to share their e-mail addresses.

With the e-mail addresses, Tellabs nurtured these leads via the Marketo system. Tellabs tracked the behavior of the leads. With Marketo, Stenitzer said, "We can see your footprints on the site.

And if you hit a lot of content in a short period of time, the algorithm automatically generates an e-mail to use and tells us, 'Here's a marketing qualified lead,' which we then hand off to sales."

Using the e-mail addresses in Marketo, Stenitzer was able to track whether those leads turned into actual revenue after they were handed off to sales. The tracking showed, beyond doubt, that marketing helped drive sales. Stenitzer said that between 2010 and 2012, marketing tripled the revenue that it had a hand in generating. He said the figure may be even higher, because deals can take 18 months or more to close in the telecom equipment business.

Tellabs also discovered other details from using data to tie together content, leads, and revenue. "We learned that almost all of our marketing-sourced sales came from North America and Europe," Stenitzer said. "We learned that marketing was much more successful in selling our optical product than in selling our mobile product. We were more well-known for our mobile product in the first place and probably less well-known for our optical product—but we could move the needle more in optical."

He added that marketing helped more with customers outside of Tellabs' traditional telecom market. "A lot of the sales leads created through our content and demand gen were not coming from the enterprise," Stenitzer said. "They were coming from electrical utilities. They were coming from local governments, like county governments. There wasn't a salesforce dedicated to these kinds of customers."

The Tellabs story shows that large corporations (Tellabs had revenue of $1.1 billion in 2013, the year it was acquired by Marlin Equity Partners) can implement data-driven marketing principles. But many observers believe it's harder for big companies to embrace big data, because they have so many legacy systems. Marketers can be overwhelmed by the data contained in different silos and the prospect of somehow merging all of this data into a single system. The cost, in time and money, of unraveling what Lisa Arthur, CMO of Teradata Marketing Applications, a marketer of integrated marketing management solutions, calls "the big data hairball" can be daunting.

At smaller companies, the process of becoming a data-driven business can be easier. In the big data age, being nimble can also give smaller companies an advantage.

"The small to middle-sized companies are in the best position to do so, because they have a single unified marketing team," said Chris Robison, general manager of the direct business at Poppin, an office supplies e-commerce start-up. He was previously senior director of product and strategy at marketing technology vendor Adobe Systems.

"You can really be David to the big companies' Goliath by leveraging data effectively," Brian Kardon, CMO of Lattice Engines, said. "You can beat much bigger, well-funded companies if you're able to harness that data. It's a way to get an amplifier effect to do amazing things. Big data could be the key for a lot of smaller companies, giving them a much better return on their marketing dollar. It's a great leveler."

If embracing big data is easier at smaller companies, at start-ups the process can be easier still. Bill Macaitis, former CMO at Zendesk, which markets cloud-based customer service software, had the luxury of building a data-driven marketing team essentially from scratch when he joined the company in 2012.

Macaitis started working in digital marketing after he graduated from the University of Illinois. Working in management positions at Salesforce.com, Fox Interactive Media, IGN Entertainment, and elsewhere, he has witnessed digital marketing evolve at an ever-quickening pace as marketers have seized the power of websites, search, social, and mobile.

But even as marketers have taken advantage of these new digital tools, they have grappled with how to continue to make the most of embedded legacy marketing tactics, such as media buying, brochures, and trade shows. So Macaitis was intrigued in 2012 when he took the CMO job at Zendesk, because the job would offer an unusual opportunity to start a new digital marketing organization from the ground up—without any legacy silos. "The primary reason I came there was they didn't really have a big marketing organization," he said. "It's really kind of a rare chance to build a marketing org almost from scratch. It's a new age marketing organization that doesn't have any traditional silos. . . . I came to build the most advanced, sophisticated B2B marketing team ever."

In building the organization he envisioned, Macaitis had four words as his foundation: data driven, customer focused. "I'm a 100 percent data-driven, customer-focused believer," he said. "I think those four words really sum up the new paradigm."

When creating his marketing department at Zendesk, Macaitis focused on two key elements: content marketing and analytics. "We made a couple of big investments," he said. "One of the first ones was we created a big content team. We hired six full-time content people. All they do is create content left and right."

On the face of it, content seems unrelated to data-driven marketing. But Macaitis says that content is crucial to understanding how prospects are self-educating as they move through the buyer's journey, most of which now takes place online. Analyzing individual content pieces can provide insight into which ones are the most influential in driving prospects through the marketing funnel. "Which ones drove the most leads?" Macaitis asks his team about the content it creates. "Which ones actually drove the most pipeline? Which ones helped accelerate the deal velocity? Which ones allowed us to get the giant, big deal that made our quarter? There are interesting lessons in it, and it's not an arbitrary process or a philosophical call."

In addition to building the content team, Macaitis hired a large analytics crew. This group is in charge of constructing Zendesk's marketing stack, which now includes more than 30 different kinds of software such as Optimizely and Convertro. "They are in charge of all the attribution, the reporting, a lot of the insight," he said. "They are in charge of training the rest of the team to use the tools. They make sure we are leveraging all the data out there. We built out a pretty sophisticated marketing technology stack."

The ability to properly attribute what marketing tactics are accelerating prospects through the funnel is vital. The attribution software that Zendesk uses, Convertro, is the foundation of the stack, Macaitis said. This software, combined with the rest of Zendesk's marketing stack, enables the company to track the impact of marketing on prospects long before they ever share an e-mail address.

"Attribution, especially here in B2B marketing, is so important," Macaitis said, "because people don't really understand how much of that research comes in before a person arrives at your site. . . . You come across prospects 10, 20, 30 times before they ever become a lead. Marketers say, 'Oh, it's a long sales cycle. From the minute prospects become a lead until we close them, it's three months.' But you know there's another three months before that, where the prospect is anonymously researching your company and seeing you again and again. . . . We have always thought that the average time someone spent interacting with a brand before they formally announce themselves was pretty long. Attribution actually confirms it. We saw these 10, 20, 30 clickstreams. People interacting with a display ad or seeing a display, display, display. Then social paid, then social organic. And branded, nonbranded."

Macaitis also uses the Net Promoter Score (NPS), which is another aspect of Zendesk's data-driven, customer-focused marketing approach. NPS asks customers the likelihood, on a scale of 0 to 10, of whether they would recommend the company to their friends or colleagues. If the customer answers 9 or 10, the customer is a promoter. Those who answer 7 or 8 are considered neutral. An answer of 6 or below is considered a detractor.

In its use of NPS, Zendesk digs a little deeper, asking customers what attributes of the company influenced their likelihood to recommend the company. Macaitis said the NPS survey has helped Zendesk by demonstrating the importance of customer service, which has helped the company in marketing its customer service software.

"We classified the top five reasons they recommend us, and the number two reason was: 'I had a great experience with one of your support people, and because of that, I am much more likely to recommend you,'" Macaitis said. "That was amazing, because here you have the power of data. Marketing should be saying, 'If I want to grow my organization, if I want to get more leads . . . I actually should be arguing for more support people.'"

After installing his marketing team at Zendesk, Macaitis is more convinced than ever about the power of the data-driven, customer-focused approach. He said marketers who aren't following this path are "underestimating the power of data, the power of targeting, the power of the marketing tech stack and what it can do."

He adds, "When I tell people that we can in real time know every single visitor when they arrive on our site and what company type they are from, and that we can target specific titles or regions or individual companies, they're blown away."

Eleven Principles to Follow When Bringing Big Data into Your Business

Whether you're at a large company or a small company, there is some basic advice that applies to every size company when taking those first steps to make your business more data driven. Here are 11 principles to keep in mind when bringing big data into your business.

Focus on the Customer to Determine What Questions You Want Your Data to Answer

The best companies have a data-driven focus on the customer. These companies use data to understand their customers, which, in turn, gives them a better understanding of prospects.

A key to using data efficiently is to know what you want to know about your customers and prospects. Look for the signal amid the noise. Knowing their attributes and how they behave online can move the needle when it comes to revenue and profits.

"The most important thing when you're dealing with big data is what are the questions you're trying to answer," Citrix's Sosa said.

When targeting prospects, what are their important characteristics? Their company size? Geographic location? Job title or job function? Industry? When prospects visit your website, what behaviors indicate a readiness to buy? Downloading certain white papers? Viewing product data sheets? Spending time on the pricing information?

When analyzing customers, what characteristics do your best customers have in common, and where can you find more of them? What behaviors indicate a likelihood of customers switching to a competitor, and what steps can you take to retain them?

To understand prospects, Ruth P. Stevens, president of marketing consulting firm eMarketing Strategy, said the key is digging into the buyer's journey. "It's about analyzing the buying process of your target audience," she said, adding, "The first step is to figure out what it is that you need to measure, and in order to do that you need to understand what are your goals. Are you going to measure based on leads generated? Are you going to measure based on sales or revenue?"

It's Big Data, but Start Small

When incorporating big data into your processes, think little triggers. The amount of data that the average company has the potential to collect through its website alone can be overwhelming. For each website visitor, a company could collect data on that visitor's demographics (based on her cookie), could identify whether she is a repeat visitor, could track her onsite behavior, and could analyze what drove her to the site—among many other pieces of information.

The key is to determine what precise pieces of data about the customer are most important to your business goals. "You can't take on everything at once," Sosa said. "Look for the small wins."

Starting small makes sense for several reasons. First, it won't tax your technology budget. Second, it enables you to build the processes around big data slowly and in a controlled fashion. And third, it gives you the opportunity to have small wins using data that can ultimately earn you buy-in—and budget allocations—from the decision makers.

Implementing small but impactful data-driven programs can be deceptively simple. In fact, some of the easiest steps can be overlooked. In a *Harvard Business Review* guest blog post on May 22, 2014, "Why Websites Still Can't Predict Exactly What You Want," Kaiser Fung, a statistician for Vimeo, said that personalization based on your past website behavior is a simple step ignored by even the best companies.

He writes that FreshDirect, an online grocer he uses, is taking simple steps to get personalization right: "If you search for a product you have purchased in the past, FreshDirect lists those items first, labeling them 'Your Fave.' When I look for 'water,' Poland Spring shows up at the top of the list; if I search 'Poland Spring,' the computer knows my standard order of a six-pack of one-gallon containers." That's the kind of personalization that leads to better customer service.

Don't Bet Everything on Technology

Don't get us wrong. Selecting the right technology is critical, but don't start with technology. Don't get your heart set, for instance, on using a data management platform before you analyze the buyer's journey, your customer's needs, and your company culture.

"If you start throwing technology at it, you are missing the human element, which is critical," Teradata Marketing Applications' Arthur said. "The human element means there is a buyer with a face, with a need. My first caution is, regardless of the size of the company, do not start with the technology. That is a recipe for disaster. You have to start with the interaction strategy, the buyer's journey."

However, some observers advise that certain baseline resources can be considered essential. For instance, Brian Krause, vice president of marketing and communications at Molex, said, "There are some specific needs. One is an e-mail database. Two is a very focused lead generation team that is very close to the sales organization."

Richard Roberts, senior vice president of sales and marketing for BusinessOnline, a B2B digital marketing agency, said, "The first step is absolutely implementing the right customer data management capabilities for your company." At the heart of this is an analytics tool—even something free such as Google Analytics—that can give any company insight into its website traffic and how tactics like paid search and display are influencing that traffic.

Hire the Right People

When considering your marketing staff, think less about raiding art schools and more about setting up a recruiting booth at a *Star Trek* convention. Embracing big data means hiring more mathematicians, data scientists, and chief marketing technologists. Or put more simply, hire people who are very comfortable with numbers and spreadsheets and are curious enough to want to understand the underlying details of what is driving success.

The marketing department still needs creative people, but it also demands analytical people who can provide insights so the creative team stays on track. Matt Ackley, CMO and senior vice president of product at Marin Software, identified two hurdles to building a data-driven marketing team. "The challenge becomes two bullets," he said. "One is getting access to the data, and then the second piece is finding the analytics people who can do something with the data."

Getting those analytics people, however, may be easier said than done. There is an increasing demand for their services. "Google and Amazon can afford to attract and pay the experts on this stuff," BusinessOnline's Roberts said. "But it's really hard to find and afford these people. The average B2B company is not going to be able to cost-justify a senior analytics person, because you're likely talking around six figures. If it's a data architect, then you're going to be paying him what you pay your VP of marketing."

Maintain Some Control of the Technology Piece

Almost every marketing chief has experienced the frustration of being at the mercy of the information technology department to get a sentence modified on the corporate website. But that is changing quickly. Marketers are demanding that new technologies be accessible by their staffers and not just IT.

Technology is now an integral part of marketing. The user experience on a company website is just as important as the company tagline. Marketing must at the very least share control of the technology that is increasingly a part of its responsibilities.

"I strongly believe every marketing organization should have a technical arm that reports to the marketing organization, and every marketing organization should have an analytics group that is dedicated or reports to the marketing organization," Marin Software's Ackley said.

Measure, Measure, and Measure Some More

In addition to providing insights into prospects and customers, big data can tell marketers which of their programs are working—and which are not. The enhanced measurement capabilities of digital marketing and the ease of A/B testing in digital environments enable marketers to put more money behind the most effective programs.

Additionally, digital programs can be measured essentially in real time. Marketers need to monitor their campaigns on a weekly, daily, or even hourly basis. Glenn Gow, president of the marketing agency Crimson Marketing, said, "You need a dashboard mentality."

In the past, measurement was limited and slow. Marketers had a difficult time, for instance, measuring the impact of a print advertising campaign on revenue. They might get a creative award for it, but even that took months.

The rise of marketing technology systems has changed that irrevocably. Joe Payne, the former CEO of Eloqua, described this change: "Today we want to look at the effectiveness. How many people opened the campaign? How much time did they engage with it? How many people responded? Three weeks later, how many people we closed business with were touched by that campaign? There are lots of different ways to measure marketing, but now we can measure effectiveness. And so what you're going to see is the sophistication of the user and the use of the marketing technology systems come together for the next two years, and you're going to see pretty much everybody adopting these systems."

Stay on Top of Your Data and the Processes Around That Data

With new technologies appearing almost every day, it can be overwhelming for traditional CMOs, who are tempted to cede control of, say, the marketing automation software to someone from the millennial generation or a digital native.

Payne described the situation this way: "All too often the CMO will say, 'I let Jennie handle that.' But Jennie is new and doesn't know how to measure the effectiveness of marketing in general. And since Johnny the CMO didn't understand how the technology works, he just froze and said, 'I don't deal with that.'"

There is a danger in this approach, because technology is inextricably linked with marketing's goals. Strategy and software are bound together: the CMO must understand both.

Conduct a Data Audit and Strive to Integrate Data Silos

Many companies are already collecting more data than they know what to do with and are not using that data effectively. A data audit can help them identify what data they have access to and give them a better handle on what data they actually need to boost revenue and profits.

"It is good to also take stock of all the sources of data that you have available, because most people overlook the fact that they have tons of behavioral data already that can be leveraged—but they don't incorporate it or send it to the right places," Citrix's Sosa said.

At most companies, much of this data sits in separate silos. Customer service has different data on the customer than sales has, which has different data than marketing, which has different data than the e-commerce platform, which has different data than a company's advertising agency.

Many marketers (and marketing technology vendors) envision being able to centralize this data, now contained in a variety of silos, into a single database that will give a complete or 360-degree view of the customer.

All of this is a noble goal but may, for the time being, be beyond the reach of most companies and most budgets. "We as marketers and we as technology providers are both a long way off from making that vision a reality for most companies. The promise is there, but it comes down to, 'How do I do this in a scalable and cost-effective fashion?' It is all about measuring the return on investment," said Poppin's Robison.

Cooperate with IT, Sales, Human Resources, and Other Stakeholders

Start small, but think big. Start with small data-driven projects but have an eye on using data to improve not only marketing performance but the entire business. To accomplish this big goal, a marketing team will need buy-in from other departments. At a smaller company this is often easy, but at larger companies it can be one of the most difficult barriers to change.

A 2014 IBM report, "Stepping Up to the Challenge: CMO Insights from the Global C-Suite Study," advises CMOs to "get the CIO on your side." Having the CIO on board is a necessity for building out the technology necessary to make the most effective use of big data. Sales must be on board to make sure marketing qualified leads are taken seriously. And human resources must be on board to help marketing find the data-oriented employees necessary to take full advantage of big data.

"The technology in many cases actually works pretty well," Poppin's Robison said. "Now the biggest barrier that I've seen is related to the business management and the process change management that is required to execute data-driven integrated marketing."

Practice Good Data Hygiene

You'd think that keeping data in a marketing database up-to-date would be a straightforward task. But it's not—especially when you consider that one in five businesses changes a postal address every year.

A report by NetProspex, a data vendor catering to marketing, called "The State of Marketing Data," found that 88 percent of business databases were lacking very basic data, such as the prospect's industry, company revenues, and number of employees. An astonishing 64 percent of records did not include a phone number.

This kind of information is critical for marketers and salespeople looking to start conversations with prospects. In the digital age, databases are essential, and it is essential that they are kept up-to-date. "Database quality now has an unprecedented impact on the success of our marketing campaigns," Michael Bird, CEO of

NetProspex, wrote in the report. "Simply put: data drives revenue for your company."

To ensure that these databases are as productive as possible, marketers must maintain good data hygiene. In a column, eMarketing Strategy's Stevens outlined a list of five steps for cleaner data:

1. Make sure your data entry team is keying in data accurately in the first place. Make the data-entry team a priority.
2. Incentivize your sales team, call center squad, and other customer-facing employees to regularly request updated contact information and other data from the customers they encounter.
3. Use available software, such as Trillium, to streamline the process of cleansing, correcting, and appending e-mail and postal addresses.
4. Allow customers access to their records, so they can help keep them accurate. Consider offering discounts as an incentive for customers to participate.
5. Regularly contact customers, either via phone or e-mail, to update records. This approach is critical with the most important accounts.

Develop a Road Map, but Anticipate Detours

Embracing big data at most companies can require a massive transformation. It can involve a culture shift, new technologies and processes, and the hiring of different personnel.

This transformation means big plans, and it may require outside consultants to help you map a strategy, choose the right technologies, and make all the right moves. But be careful not to slavishly adhere to a blueprint that has worked for other companies. Big data is not about keeping pace; it's about building a big—and unique—advantage.

"Don't be a cookie cutter," said Heather Zynczak, CMO of Domo. "Get your data in place, so that you can measure and do things outside the box and do things that are wildly different. That will leapfrog you over the competition. There's not a cookie-cutter approach to marketing, because then you're only going to be as good as your peers."

CHAPTER 10

Measurement, Testing, and Attribution

It's an ancient complaint that it is difficult, if not impossible, to tell if advertising works—even though advertising has always been measured in some fashion. When ads ran, clients might offer their opinions on the creative side: thumbs up or thumbs down. Maybe the phone rang a little more often. There might be more sales opportunities—maybe, maybe not. And in some cases, revenue increased.

Historically, large marketers would attempt to advertise in single geographic locations and measure lift in revenue per store or similar metrics to see if the advertising was creating any measurable difference in a market where the population was exposed to the ads, compared to other markets where there was no exposure. But unless the test was very well designed, it was still often hard to tell if it was the advertising that was actually causing these results.

But now, with advanced uses of data, marketers and their advertising agency counterparts can tie marketing and advertising to revenue more tightly and reliably than ever before. With the right data, the right technology, and the right approach, marketers can test various initiatives, measure responses, and focus efforts on those initiatives that contribute directly to increased revenue.

Data has also enabled a more sophisticated and holistic view of how marketing works. Different marketing initiatives have different objectives. A branding campaign, for instance, generally delivers different outcomes than a paid search campaign or an e-mail newsletter. And because they have different goals, they are measured differently. As Marc Yasuda, head of business-to-business (B2B) sales enablement at LinkedIn, is fond of pointing out, marketing and the measurement of it are analogous to a baseball lineup. The leadoff hitter and the cleanup hitter have different jobs. The leadoff hitter's job is to get on base any way possible—bunt, infield single, walk. The cleanup hitter's job is to drive in runs, often with extra-base hits and home runs.

So it would be foolish to measure the leadoff hitter and the cleanup hitter with the same statistics. You wouldn't measure a leadoff hitter by runs batted in or home runs, just as you wouldn't measure a cleanup hitter by on-base percentage or stolen bases. To do so would be to seriously misoptimize the players needed to generate runs in baseball, and losses would quickly result.

It's similar in marketing. Branding campaigns should be judged by whether they induce qualified prospects to visit your website or enter the top of your marketing funnel and how engaged those prospects become. And other lead-generation tactics, such as paid search, should be judged by the number of leads they generate.

In combination with this enlightened approach to metrics, data allows more precise measurement of marketing programs. It has enabled real-time testing of creative concepts. And it delivers sophisticated and accurate attribution models that can tell which tactics contribute most to an actual sale.

Data and Measurement

With the ability to measure the efficacy of various marketing initiatives along with a staff of analytics-savvy marketers, companies are able to track marketing results precisely.

ClearSlide, a sales enablement software company, is a great example of a company collecting and analyzing various sources of data to optimize their business offering. Traditionally, the creative side has been divorced from metrics. Art directors designed from their gut, based on their personal sense of what looked good—what was attractive. Now, at ClearSlide, metrics heavily influence how, for instance, the company redesigned its website.

ClearSlide is able to measure aspects of its marketing efforts that were, in the past, quite difficult to gauge. The company is able to measure even complicated marketing initiatives, which have historically been difficult or impossible to measure in any meaningful way.

Kathryn Frengs, director of marketing communications at ClearSlide, has a unique approach to measuring her company's programs.

The effectiveness of public relations (PR) initiatives has always been difficult to gauge. It has been a qualitative tactic, despite attempts to measure clips and line inches of copy a company received in online or traditional media. Once Frengs became involved in ClearSlide's public relations initiatives, she quickly developed a format for measuring monthly performance of the PR program:

"We created a metrics-based measurement tool that gives us the ability to gauge the quality of the mention we get while also determining the impact of the hit compared against a target list of publications," Frengs said. "It's a little complicated, but at the end the net is that it assigns a score to each media hit that we can then use to tabulate monthly and quarterly scores and have specific metrics that we work toward in PR."

Based on a number of factors in this system, Frengs tabulates the impact of the company's PR efforts. Getting a mention in a blog post gets fewer points than getting a mention in a tech publication, which gets fewer points than getting a mention in a general business magazine. If the story includes a quote from a ClearSlide spokesperson, it also generates positive points. And, of course, positive stories get more points than neutral or negative pieces. The ClearSlide marketing team presents a chart to the CEO and the board, all of whom like numbers.

ClearSlide also analyzed data when making changes to its corporate website. "Our previous website had three buttons in the middle of the home page: 'Watch Demo,' 'Learn More,' and 'Get Started.' In the upper right-hand corner was a button that read, 'Free Trial,'" Frengs said. "Analytics showed that 'Watch Demo' and 'Free Trial' were the two most heavily clicked buttons on the page." So ClearSlide eliminated the "Learn More" and "Get Started" buttons, moved the "Free Trial" option front and center, and put a video on the front page complete with a YouTube-style play button superimposed on it. As expected, results went up.

Of course, the redesign didn't end there. ClearSlide now uses analytics to analyze its traffic continually as part of an effort to optimize the site's design. It also regularly employs A/B testing to find incremental design improvements.

Measuring the Power of Display Ads

In addition to using data to influence website design and measure PR performance, ClearSlide also uses data to improve performance of its advertising campaigns. Whether TV, print, radio, or online, advertising campaigns have always been notoriously difficult to measure. In the past, a print campaign might cause a surge in phone calls, but marketers found it hard to determine whether the ad campaigns were driving the right leads to the company.

In its online display advertising, ClearSlide uses Bizo's technology to serve online display ads only to its target audience—in this case primarily the business demographic of sales executives. If you're not a sales executive, it's unlikely that you will see any of ClearSlide's display ads.

The online display ads drove an increase in web traffic by that key target group. "We saw a 145 percent increase to our website by visitors who were also VPs of sales for their organizations," Frengs said. "Huge. That's not anything we would have found anywhere else. What was really great, too, is we were able to drill down and see all of the people that Bizo introduced to our website. They were going to nearly 100 percent more pages than visitors who hadn't been exposed to the display ads; they were spending almost 100 percent more time on our website than just the typical visitor from somewhere else."

Data and Testing

Marketers have always had the opportunity to test the efficacy of their creative campaigns. The big advertising agencies used focus groups to assess how audiences would respond to various TV spots. Still, focus groups are inherently limited: they generally accommodate only a handful of people and only account for opinions, not actual behaviors or purchases.

The rise of digital marketing along with the concurrent rise of data analytics have made testing marketing at scale feasible. Marketers can quickly A/B test almost any digital initiative. They can test e-mail subject lines against each other. They can test newsletter calls to action. They can test paid search ad headlines. They can do any of these, get virtually immediate feedback, and can then optimize with the better-performing option.

Display advertising is another marketing strategy where A/B testing can vastly improve the results of a marketing initiative. Bizo helps clients test their ad creative concepts: ad sizes, headlines, colors, calls to action, visuals, and more. The idea is to optimize the efficacy of the campaign by ensuring it reaches the broadest target audience with the most effective message and ad.

This testing is key, because marketers no longer have to rely on their gut feeling for guessing how campaigns will perform. It can be hard to predict which creative concept will perform better. In the following display ad examples, one of the options performed far better than the other. See if you can make the correct call (Figures 10.1 and 10.2).

Test No. 1: MyCase

Target Audience: Lawyers
Metric: Conversions

A

B

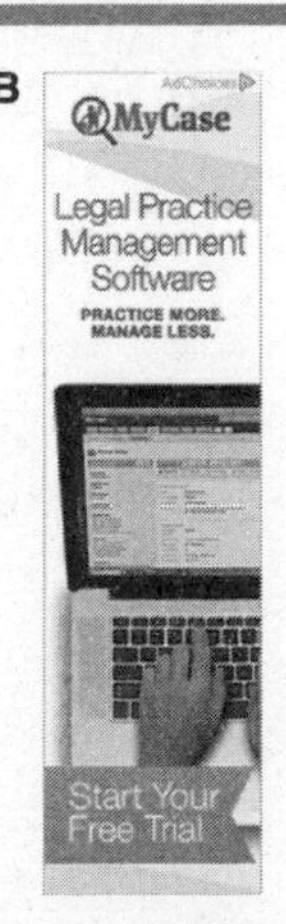

FIGURE 10.1 MyCase Ads

Ad A delivered the stronger performance with a conversion rate that was 1.6 times higher than Ad B. (See Figure 10.1.) The difference in performance appears to be Ad A's focus on benefits. Ad A clearly identifies the legal practice software as web-based and presents the software as easy to use, enabling prospects to work from anywhere.

Test No. 2: Better Business Bureau

Target Audience: **Executives**
Metric: **Conversions**

FIGURE 10.2 Better Business Bureau Ads

Ad B delivered 2.4 times more leads even though the only difference was the call to action. (See Figure 10.2.) "You should register your business" may have sounded like less hassle than "You should apply for accreditation," or maybe people just didn't know what accreditation really meant.

The point is, it's hard to tell exactly why one ad outperformed another. Ad performance is hard to predict, but it doesn't matter if you have the right A/B testing in place.

Data and Attribution

Finding an attribution model—a system that accurately attributes the contribution made by each and every one of a company's marketing tactics to leads and to revenue—is the holy grail for data-driven marketers. Some marketers are very close to realizing a model that works, but most marketers are using primitive forms of attribution at best, which typically place too much value on lower-funnel, last-click tactics and result in many companies allocating too much of their budgets on the wrong efforts.

Richard Roberts, senior vice president of sales and marketing at B2B digital marketing agency BusinessOnline, defines attribution this way: "allocating proportional credit to all marketing communications across all channels that ultimately lead to the desired customer action."

There are three basic attribution models.

The first is *last-click attribution*. This model gives 100 percent of the credit for a conversion or a sale to the last marketing element the prospect interacted with. Oftentimes that marketing element is a lower-funnel tactic, such as e-mail or paid search. The deficiency in this model is that it gives too much credit to the lower funnel without recognizing the contribution made by branding efforts that got the prospect in the funnel in the first place or nurturing and education efforts that moved the prospect deeper into the funnel. Or, to return to the baseball analogy, this would be like giving a grand-slam home run hitter credit for all four runs even though the three previous batters needed to get on base to score when the fourth batter knocked it out of the park.

Roberts doesn't find last-click attribution to provide an accurate picture of customer behavior, because it ignores much of the buyer's journey and other reasons. "It's the most common approach, but we at BusinessOnline don't even really categorize this as attribution, in fact," he said. "We find it can do more harm than good by overvaluing certain types of interactions."

The second type of attribution model is *rules-based attribution*. With this model, a marketer assigns a certain value to particular tactics based on predetermined rules. For a prospect that interacted with three different tactics before becoming a customer, a marketer might assign each tactic equal credit. If that prospect interacted with display, e-mail, and search, each of the tactics would be credited with driving one-third of that customer's revenue. While this approach is more sophisticated than last-click attribution, rules-based attribution often mirrors a marketer's own prejudices about what tactics work rather than reflecting the actual influence of various tactics.

"This kind of rules-based approach doesn't really have the analytical rigor that we'd like and may actually not be much of a better approach than the first one—the single touch kind of measurement," Roberts said.

The third and most accurate attribution model is *algorithmic attribution*. "The third approach assigns values to each interaction based on statistical regression or probabilistic models," Roberts said. "These data-driven models typically provide the most accurate picture of the customer journey."

In part, this method examines how a marketing tactic contributes to conversions, leads, and revenue by examining data from ad platforms, search engine optimization (SEO) tools, web analytics, paid search tools, marketing automation software, customer relationship management (CRM) systems, social measurement tools, and even offline events and tactics (such as TV, print, or radio ads). Because most of these tools are digital, this performance can be examined at scale and essentially in real time.

This kind of attribution requires some grunt work, some statistical know-how, and an openness to data. Roberts said some marketers aren't always comfortable with the conclusions this kind of attribution model reaches. "Sometimes marketers actually are uncomfortable with knowing the truth—with having to give up their data to a model they don't understand and not being able to add their gut feeling input on decisions," he said. "When I say uncomfortable with the truth, I mean sometimes we'll have results come out of these stat-driven models, and our clients just won't like it. They'll say, 'Well, geez, I just feel like, you know, such and such has been my workhorse and you're suggesting that it's a complete waste of money. I just don't believe that.'" The truth—in marketing as in life—can often be a hard pill to swallow, and this can be a significant reason why some organizations don't drive hard toward data-driven models.

But Roberts is a believer. "It gives you a powerful data-backed methodology for looking back on anonymous visitor activity and then linking it to known leads or sales," he said.

The first step in algorithmic attribution is identifying anonymous visitors to a corporate website. These visitors can be identified with a cookie or other tracking technology with the goal of tracking their path to purchase.

"Once those visitors who were anonymous early in their journey become known, when they register to download something or they interact with your sales team, it gives you a full picture and ultimately the ability to measure which activities, campaigns, or even content assets are best leading to sales," he said. "It allows you to optimize programs based on revenue rather than front-end metrics, like visits or leads."

To build this statistical attribution model, a company would look back on its marketing data and correlate all of the activities that drove sales. The company looks back for a time period equivalent to its typical buyer's journey—as long as 18 months or two years for some companies. Based on the data, the company assigns higher values to the marketing tactics that are meaningful—the ones that drove conversions or revenue or both.

This kind of attribution is not theory. It is in practice right now.

At DocuSign, Inc., which provides digital transaction management services, the marketing team is using a fairly sophisticated attribution model. The company generates about 130,000 leads per quarter. DocuSign has built a system that scores leads, ties them to a particular campaign or tactic, monitors conversion rates, and connects the leads to revenue. Ultimately, this approach enables DocuSign to prioritize specific leads, so that salespeople are following up with only those most likely to make a purchase. "It's really important that we are measuring the leads that come in effectively, so we can prioritize whom to talk to, and so we can make it a lot more efficient for our sales team," Meagen Eisenberg, vice president of customer marketing at DocuSign, said.

She explained the philosophy behind DocuSign's approach: "This is a closed-loop model. We score it. We tie it to a campaign. If it's converting, we see that in the results, and we'll adjust the score accordingly. It's all about continual improvement and the learnings that come with that. Lastly, what really makes marketers today is their ability to measure and show the attribution and spend effectively."

The system also analyzes leads based on their business demographics and their level of engagement. "We're taking that knowledge and putting it back into our scoring systems. So we iterate on our lead scoring model at least once a quarter," Eisenberg said.

DocuSign acts quickly to kill underperforming campaigns. "If I see a program or spend not working, I'm going to either stop it midcampaign or reallocate or both," Eisenberg said. "Then I am going to double down on the ones that are working."

Eisenberg is extremely confident in the capability of data-driven marketing and solid attribution models to prove that online marketing spending is working. "I feel pretty confident in the metrics, and the tracking, and the technology we have today to prove what spend is working and what spend is not when it comes to online marketing and am excited to see the improvements that technology will bring," she said.

Attribution's Big Day

Some marketers build attribution models on their own, but they don't have to. Attribution software companies such as Adometry, Convertro, and VisualIQ have developed systems to help marketers build relevant attribution models for their own businesses. This particular segment of the marketing space proved quite attractive to big players in media and marketing technology, as demonstrated by America Online (AOL) acquiring Convertro, and Google acquiring Adometry on the exact same day: May 6, 2014.

Jeff Zwelling helped found Convertro in 2009 after selling an e-commerce company called YLighting. Zwelling said that his e-commerce company owed part of its success to an attribution model it had built to ensure the efficiency of its own marketing spending. He decided to build a new company, which became Convertro, around this marketing and optimization software.

Previously, marketers analyzed their spend using a mixed-media model, which finds correlations between marketing spending and business outcomes, such as leads or revenue. Regression analytics finds the correlation between a marketing tactic and revenue, for instance. This correlation is then tested experimentally by stopping the tactic for a period and then seeing whether revenue declines. If it does, then the impact of the tactic is proven.

This kind of approach was available before the digital age to measure the impact of television advertising. Convertro, however, moves far beyond this approach to measuring marketing impact. Using the power and speed of big data, Convertro allows marketers to get information about what's working that is much more granular, updated daily rather than weekly or monthly, and eminently actionable.

In the digital world, it is possible to measure the impact (or lack of impact) of a display ad campaign, for instance, or the performance of search, e-mail, and other digital tactics almost immediately. "We have near real-time ability to capture both the impression data (those are clicks and views), as well as the spend data (how much you spent on it), and most importantly, attribute that to an individual user, so that you can see what they were exposed to and what the outcome was as well as all the people who you exposed it to that didn't convert," Zwelling said.

From Convertro's software, Zwelling said he has learned some key lessons. First, online display advertising works. So do TV spots on long tail cable TV—such as running an ad on ESPN2 at four o'clock in the afternoon for under $1,000—which works very well. Affiliate marketing, on the other hand, doesn't work at all. "All the coupon sites are a total waste of money for advertisers," Zwelling said. "You're going to get those sales anyway without paying commission to someone to show a coupon that you're actually using to reduce your margin."

He said not everyone is convinced by what Convertro's software has shown about the relative effectiveness of various marketing strategies. Some people, for instance, refuse to believe that online video isn't an effective marketing strategy, mainly because most people, especially baby boomers with money to spend, haven't yet cut the cable cord. But Zwelling said marketers with direct response (DR) backgrounds are true believers in his attribution software. "DR guys embrace the data, because all they care about is making money," Zwelling said. "They don't have any jobs to protect. They don't have any relationships they want to protect. They're not driven by demons; they're just driven by money."

Zwelling predicted, however, that it won't be long before many more marketers join the DR guys to become believers in attribution models like the one used by Convertro. "From my perspective, it all changed May 6," Zwelling said. "When Google announced they bought our competition and AOL bought us, for all intents and purposes that was the end of last-click attribution."

Paul Pellman was the CEO of Adometry, and after Google's acquisition of the company, he is now director/head of Adometry at Google. Like Convertro's Zwelling, Pellman says that his company's attribution model builds on the measurement methods pioneered by direct mailers, but uses hundreds of millions, or even billions, of interactions. "If you think about the direct mail and direct response industry 20 years ago before there was an Internet, the benefit of direct marketing is you get very accurately measured impact when you're mailing 2 million pieces of mail," Pellman said. "You get a certain amount of them back who convert, and you can very accurately calculate the cost per action of the impact of your marketing."

In the digital space, Adometry has a more sophisticated approach, only now with marketers who can buy billions of touch points per month to reach their target audience. "The concept of attribution is to use a data-driven methodology to very precisely allocate credit across this stream of media that users are seeing, so that marketers can get better clarity of what's really driving success," Pellman said.

In working with its clients, Adometry has learned many things about effective advertising. One key insight: "Quality of ad experience, quality of content, high-quality sites, and high-quality placements matter, and they deserve more credit than they have typically been given," Pellman said.

He also said that Adometry's data shows that display advertising and search work hand in hand. "You need to actually allocate more money into search to harvest the extra demands you have created through more effective display efforts," he said.

Pellman comes from a marketing background. He previously was, for instance, executive vice president of marketing and product at Hoover's Inc. He said, "I've seen the challenge of attribution firsthand. It's a passion of mine to use data to form better decisions that marketers can make."

Bettering attribution models is no small thing, he said. Google's deal to buy Adometry "just reinforces the value that people see in attribution," Pellman said. "We never saw it as a small problem. We saw it as a big problem, and that's why we focused on it."

As more marketers use sophisticated attribution models, Pellman fears that marketers clinging to last-click attribution will be left behind. "If you step up to a Texas hold 'em poker table, and you don't know who the sucker is, you are the sucker," Pellman said. "If all of your competitors are using data-driven attribution to help them measure marketing results, and you're not—you are the sucker."

Last-click attribution, of course, still persists, but data and the availability of sophisticated attribution models and other tools for measuring marketing performance have certainly put it—and the companies still relying on this flawed system—on notice.

CHAPTER 11

Data Can Be a Matter of Corporate Life and Death

Data is at the heart of some of the most influential concepts in business management. Authors such as Jim Collins, Geoffrey Moore, and Clayton Christensen have placed data at the center of their theories on why some businesses thrive, and why others crash and burn.

Collins, author of *Good to Great*, outlines many characteristics of companies that moved from being decent businesses to great investment performers. One characteristic: having a CEO at the helm who is a "Level 5 Executive," who builds "enduring greatness through a paradoxical blend of personal humility and professional will." These companies also have a "culture of discipline" and embrace technology, not for technology's sake but to improve the business. Another key element of what Collins called "good-to-great" companies is data-driven: they rely on an "economic denominator" that uses data to measure a key performance indicator. At Walgreens, for example, the economic denominator is profit per customer visit. For Nucor, it was profit per ton of finished steel. And for Abbott it was profit per employee.

In the philosophy of Moore, author of *Crossing the Chasm* and *Inside the Tornado: Marketing Strategies from Silicon Valley's Cutting Edge*, data is the key driver in an ever-changing world that marketers, especially in the tech sector, must constantly grapple with. Moore's law (which was actually formulated in the mid-1960s by a different Moore—Gordon Moore, the co-founder of Intel) holds that the number of transistors on a computer chip will double approximately every two years.

The result of this law's fulfillment is that the ability to process and store data becomes faster, easier, and cheaper. Progress, as evidenced by products such as smartphones and concepts such as cloud computing, happens quickly in the technology sector. The realization of Moore's law has caused immense changes in the ways data is created, processed, and stored. A typical smartphone, for instance, has a microprocessor more than 1,000 times faster than the computer that took Apollo 11 to the moon in 1969. Another example: every six hours, the NSA collects as much data as there is in the Library of Congress. The mind-boggling amounts of data that are created every day have led to paradigm shifts that have changed the way products are designed and companies launched.

Moore points to Google as an example of a business model that took advantage of a paradigm shift driven by Moore's law. "Historically, companies have been very selective about where to store data and how to process it, but now it's virtually free," he said. "You can just store everything, process everything, and it allows you to play the game entirely differently."

In his books, Moore outlines strategies for technology marketers to deal with the constant hurly-burly of data-driven innovation. At the cutting edge of the cycle, marketers who have gained early adopters of their product or service must "cross the chasm" to gain widespread mainstream acceptance. Counterintuitively, Moore recommends focusing on niche markets to build momentum to cross the chasm.

Once a product begins to gain mainstream acceptance—whether it's personal computers 30 years ago, laptops 20 years ago, or smartphones and tablets in the past decade—a buying frenzy begins, which Moore refers to as the "tornado." In this chaotic phase, the most important thing a marketer can do is simply ship product with a focus on becoming the dominant player in the market.

Moore's approach to marketing is built on the idea that the evolution of data processing makes disruption a near-constant condition. In this ever-changing world, marketers must remain vigilant about data's opportunities—and its dangers. "This train is moving faster than people appreciate. Now it's dangerous. These are existential threats, meaning if you don't react pretty damn quickly, you are coming out of the game entirely," Moore said.

Christensen's view, as described in *The Innovator's Dilemma: When New Technologies Cause Great Firms to Fall* (Harvard Business School Press, 1997), is similar. Change, often driven by data, is a constant. Products and services that challenge your business by delivering offerings that are not only cheaper but often better than your own, even if you are a market leader, are going to come along and eat away at your current business. Christensen's research encompasses businesses ranging from automotive manufacturers to steel companies to the tech sector. Companies too often fail to anticipate future customer needs. Christensen's counsel: Develop these new offerings yourself before others do. It is better to cannibalize yourself than to be eaten by your competitors.

Splice Machine, a startup aiming to disrupt the relational database management system (RDBMS) market controlled by Oracle, IBM, and Microsoft, is a current example of a company that embodies many of the theories put forward by Christensen, Moore, and Collins. At the same time, Splice Machine demonstrates the power of a business that is data-driven and customer-focused.

Monte Zweben, CEO of Splice Machine, was the CEO of Blue Martini Software, an e-commerce and marketing software company that he describes as part of the "first generation of big data companies." Using data mining and analytics, Blue Martini enabled marketers to analyze customer behavior across channels to identify which segments were performing best. More recently, Zweben is serving as a board member of Rocket Fuel, a programmatic media-buying platform. He saw how Rocket Fuel was using Hadoop, an open-source data architecture platform, to enable real-time decisions about media buying, and he saw an opportunity.

"I looked at the architecture: the system is world class," Zweben said. "This is unbelievable. But I also looked at the kind of people that Rocket Fuel had, and they had some tremendous specialists, ranging from some of the world's best Java engineers, database specialists, and Hadoop specialists. I thought to myself, 'How could an average company ever do this?'"

Zweben wanted to create something that would allow marketers to do what Blue Martini had done—analyze customers and their preferences—but to do this in real time, not hours or days after an individual customer's last interaction. The ability to interact with customers in real time is critical to many marketing executives. Zweben said one CMO told him, "In the old days, it was good enough to take last week's or last month's or even yesterday's data and try to build a model of what the customers' likes and dislikes are, but the real secret is if we know what the customer does in the last 10 minutes, then we can have a profound influence on their behavior."

So, combining the insight derived from his time on Rocket Fuel's board and the knowledge that marketers crave real-time data analysis, Zweben and his cofounders believe they have created a way for the average company, and its marketing team, to have the capability to analyze massive amounts of data in real time. The company they founded, Splice Machine, places an SQL database atop Hadoop's big data architecture, and this creation is outperforming traditional RDBMS products.

"It automatically scales," Zweben said. "It's like democratizing relational databases and making every company as powerful as Google or Yahoo! or Rocket Fuel. It's basically putting that power of distributed computing in the hands of everyone—but in a language they all understand, which is SQL."

Splice Machine's solution is faster than traditional RDBMS products, which can take minutes, hours, or even days to handle some queries. Perhaps even more important, Splice Machine is significantly less expensive than traditional RDBMS offerings.

Rob Fuller, managing director of the product innovation center at Harte Hanks, a company that maintains databases for marketers, confirmed that Splice Machine is fast and inexpensive. "We got some queries that were taking 30 minutes down to about eight minutes, so we can run those queries more often," Fuller said. "It is not about the same query running more often but more variants of that query running more often to do more data discovery—and to find more areas of opportunity to service our clients."

Fuller added, "We are not talking about huge capital investment based on commodity hardware and the license; it is very reasonable to scale it up for either storage or performance need." Fuller said that the Splice Machine is about one-tenth of the cost of a comparable Oracle database.

He said, "I would think Oracle database software certainly should be on notice."

Harte Hanks is not the only company that feels that way. "More companies are testing our ability to replace Oracle and MySQL systems every day," Zweben said.

In its founding and its ambitions, Splice Machine is attempting to write a story that is familiar to both Moore and Christensen. For Moore, Splice Machine is the product of the inevitable rise of big data and its spawning of new possibilities and new companies taking those possibilities to their logical limits. For Christensen, Splice Machine is a company using disruptive technology (in this case, scale out on commodity hardware) to deliver a more efficient and lower-cost product to take market share from entrenched industry leaders. Splice Machine is clearly taking on Oracle and other established RDBMS players, but it's unclear if the company is a threat or merely takeover bait.

While the story of Splice Machine is still being written, many other companies have ignored data-driven, customer-focused companies like Splice Machine until it was too late. Companies that don't embrace a culture of data and don't have a rigorous data-driven, customer focus are likely to find themselves grouped with once-great brands, such as Blockbuster, Digital Equipment Corporation (DEC), and Tower Records.

We have found it valuable to perform a post-mortem on some companies that faltered because they lacked a data-driven customer focus. We have also explored a cross-section of brands that are still breathing or even thriving, but, because they have not embraced a data-driven customer focus, may find themselves on life support in the future.

The Dead

If a company ignores data showing a trend that could fatally wound it, it's likely that the company will be wounded and that the wound will be fatal. DEC, Tower Records, and Borders Books & Music are prime examples of this phenomenon.

Digital Equipment Corporation

Digital Equipment Corporation (DEC), a pioneering computer manufacturer, was founded by Ken Olsen in 1957. Three years later the company introduced the first in a long line of PDP minicomputers. The innovative product, which was eventually followed by the VAX minicomputer, fueled DEC's rise by taking market share from mainframe computers. By 1988, DEC was a $14 billion company and the second-largest computer company in the world, behind IBM. But even when it seemed to be all green fields for DEC, the seeds for its demise had been sown: a decade later the company was sold to Compaq (which itself was eventually sold to Hewlett-Packard), and the DEC brand vanished.

DEC was slow to see the potential of the personal computing market. Olsen, who was DEC's CEO until 1992, famously said in 1977, "There is no reason for any individual to have a computer in his home." That quote actually refers not to PCs but to larger computers that would control an entire household, but the fact remains that DEC was slow to enter the PC market. The company eventually did develop PCs and entered the market in 1982, a year after IBM did and seven years after Apple helped establish this market.

DEC had three main problems that led to its ultimate downfall. First, it found itself faced with Christensen's "innovator's dilemma," which says innovative companies must cannibalize their own high-end products with less expensive products, even if they control the market, because if they don't their competitors or a start-up will. In "Good Days for Disruptors," an April 2009 interview with MIT's *Sloan Management Review*, Christensen said that DEC found itself in a classic innovator's trap.

"Digital Equipment Corp.," Christensen said, "had microprocessor technology, but its business model could not profitably sell a computer for less than $50,000. The technology trapped in a high-cost business model had no impact on the world, and in fact, the world ultimately killed Digital. But IBM Corp., with the very same processors at its disposal, set up a different business model in Florida that could make money at a $2,000 price point and 20 percent gross margins—and changed the world. It's a combination of the technology and business model that makes formerly complicated, expensive, inaccessible things affordable and accessible." Close attention and reaction to the data would have told DEC that it couldn't survive with the existing business model—that it was driving into a wall and it needed to course correct or it would crash.

Second, DEC wasn't customer focused. It was competitor focused. It was set on doing battle with IBM.

"There was also a slow recognition of the shift in the computer industry as Digital Equipment Corporation set their sights on IBM," Dave Goodwin and Roger Goodwin wrote in a short online history called "The Rise and Fall of Digital Equipment." "This chasing of IBM resulted in the hiring of a large number of personnel in the 80s which in turn resulted in the earnings per man being 30% less than HP."

And third, DEC did not collect and analyze data that would have informed it of this market shift. The evidence that the minicomputer market was stagnating and the PC market was surging was hiding in plain sight. And when DEC did enter the PC market, it did so after IBM and with a strategy of creating a closed operating system. Although that approach worked for Apple, it was not what the large market wanted at that time, as the triumph of Microsoft Windows in the 1990s made clear.

Blockbuster

In the 1990s and early 2000s, you couldn't walk a few city blocks without passing a Blockbuster store. The video rental chain was the

Starbucks of its era. At its peak in 2004, the company had 60,000 employees and 9,000 stores.

But Blockbuster's fall was fast. Facing competition from Netflix and Redbox, it declared bankruptcy in 2010. It was acquired by Dish Networks in 2011, which closed the remaining company-owned stores in 2014.

Many reasons contributed to Blockbuster's demise, but front and center was the fatal lack of a relentless data-driven focus on its customers. Among Blockbuster's many faults was a draconian late-fee policy, which bothered many customers, although in the short term it had minimal impact on Blockbuster's bottom line.

But when that late fee was fatefully levied against one customer, it changed the movie rental landscape forever. After being fined the exorbitant late fee of $40 on a copy of the movie *Apollo 13*, Blockbuster customer Reed Hastings decided there had to be a better way.

So in 1997 Hastings cofounded Netflix, which delivered movie DVDs to subscribers by mail. On the face of it, the Netflix idea seems to offer no great advantages over Blockbuster. The mail delivery did have convenience, and the business model included no late fees no matter how long you kept a movie, but it did not offer the immediacy of getting a movie from Blockbuster that a consumer could watch that day. In almost every other aspect, however, Netflix trumped Blockbuster, because it had a data-driven focus on the customer.

Netflix is a digital business, so it knows what its more than 33 million customers are watching—in the aggregate and as individuals. And with the Queue, where customers listed the movies and shows they wanted to watch, Netflix had a clear window into customers' future desires. It also, in the manner of Amazon.com, used this data to build a strong customer recommendation engine.

Additionally, because it was a digital business, Netflix was poised for success in the impending era of video streaming that followed—an advancement Blockbuster, of course, was not prepared for. More, because of its intimate knowledge of its customer preferences, Netflix was also able to develop a branch of the business focused on TV series production, which it did with astounding success with the debut of the 2013 television series *House of Cards*.

Netflix's conquering of Blockbuster is an amazing business story. The most amazing part, however, may be this: Blockbuster passed up the opportunity to buy Netflix for $50 million in 2000. The temptation is to think that acquisition would have saved Blockbuster from doom, but this move would have done so only if Blockbuster had adopted Netflix's data-driven customer focus—unlikely given that it would have involved a 180-degree cultural shift.

Tower Records and Borders

Tower Records and Borders experienced a similar rise and fall. Both delivered great retail experiences. Both were the kind of place where book lovers and music fans could browse the inventory for an entire day and never realize the time: fantastic atmosphere; great, broad selection; reasonable prices.

The business models of both Tower Records and Borders included a focus on the customer needs and customer experience. The focus, however, wasn't data-driven, which resulted in an outsized contribution to their downfall.

Tower Records At its peak, Tower Records, which started in Sacramento, California, had stores in virtually every major U.S. city and had outlets around the globe. In its best years, it posted revenue of more than $1 billion. As U.S. music sales plunged from $14.6 billion to $6.3 billion between 1999 and 2009, according to Forrester Research, Tower Records continued what had worked for it in the past—expansion.

Tower Records founder Russ Solomon believed that customers would never stop visiting his stores. The Internet, he said, "would never take the place of our stores."

But that strategy of expanding the number of stores failed to address what the hard data showed about Tower Records' customers. They didn't care if their music came from a store or was on a CD or vinyl record; they wanted to have access to and listen to music easily—a need being served by the new technology of downloadable MP3s and other electronic delivery systems. They wanted to share it easily, and they were willing—even eager—to visit websites such as Napster that the Recording Industry Association of America characterized as criminal enterprises that were pirating music.

Tower Records was in an ideal position to develop a solution to this problem of how to satisfy customers with downloadable music while generating revenue for the record labels creating the products it was selling. Tower had direct relationships with its customers, the record buyers, as well as with the record labels. The opportunity to build an online e-commerce engine for downloadable music was available to Tower Records, but it was Steve Jobs and Apple who seized that opportunity with the launch of the iTunes platform.

Tower Records filed for bankruptcy in 2004 and again in 2006, when the retailer finally went out of business.

Borders Books & Music In its early years Borders, which launched in Ann Arbor, Michigan, in 1971, was renowned for its advanced inventory system, but that focus eroded as the company grew.

Like Tower Records, Borders was a powerhouse brand. In 2003, the Borders Group operated more than 1,200 bookstores. The company kept expanding its brick-and-mortar stores even when it was clear that Amazon.com was taking market share and continuing to grow. Borders didn't launch its own proprietary website until 2008. Prior to that, the company was content with an affiliate relationship with Amazon.

Even after establishing its own proprietary e-commerce site, Borders wasn't able to compete with the rigorous data-driven customer focus that Amazon had established many years earlier. With its one-click ordering process and its recommendation engine algorithm, Amazon simply provided a better experience than Borders did—and you didn't even have to leave your house.

Borders declared bankruptcy in 2011.

Near-Death Experience

BlackBerry is fighting, but the rise of touchscreen phones with the iOS and Android operating systems cut quickly into the company's market share. BlackBerry didn't react to the customer adoption data that showed its competitors making great gains until it was almost too late.

BlackBerry, formerly Research in Motion, began manufacturing smartphones in 2000, and it was the dominant smartphone player after the turn of the century, with its user base in the United States peaking in 2010 with about 21 million users, according to comScore figures. In the wake of the introduction of the first iPhone in 2007, its market share began to erode slowly. With its physical keyboard built right into the phone, BlackBerry devices were elegant and effective e-mail machines—perfect for salespeople, investment bankers, and lawyers. The only problem was that when a BlackBerry user tried to use apps or surf the Internet, the BlackBerry wasn't as elegant or effective.

With its iPhone launch, Apple attacked BlackBerry's weak points. The iPhone could make phone calls you could actually hear (even though they often dropped because of the high usage volumes driven by the popularity of the iPhone on its then dedicated AT&T network). It delivered better Internet access. And it fostered an app environment that transformed how consumers (and developers) perceived the mobile opportunity.

Consumers loved the iPhone, which sold its 1 millionth unit just 74 days after its unveiling. Apple took a customer-centric approach to building the iPhone. In Walter Isaacson's biography, *Steve Jobs* (Simon & Schuster, 2011), he writes that Jobs "had noted something odd about the cell phones on the market: They all stank, just like the portable music players used to [before the iPod]." So drawing on the data that the iPod had sold 20 million units in 2005 and there were 825 million cell phones in use at that time, Jobs decided to embark on the iPhone project.

Once the iPhone hit the market, BlackBerry, for its part, did not recognize the data that indicated high adoption rates of the iPhone. BlackBerry dismissed the touch screen as a niche product that would not cut into what it thought was its unassailable market share among businesses. But the bring your own device (BYOD) phenomenon demonstrated that the iPhone (and soon Google's Android phone) was hacking away at BlackBerry's grip on the business market.

BlackBerry made a number of mistakes, but its primary one was not adapting the business based on the data indicating that the strong growth of the iPhone would cut into its market share. BlackBerry also didn't take a strong enough customer focus and was satisfied with building excellent e-mail machines but allowing the phone reception and web surfing aspects of its product to be mediocre at best.

BlackBerry is building better products now. Its phones get great reviews, but the damage to the brand incurred by Apple and Android leapfrogging its products may have been fatal. In 2014, BlackBerry's web usage in North America fell to fourth behind Android, Apple, and Microsoft.

Culture Clash

The data has long shown that newspapers are struggling in the digital age, especially for advertising dollars. The data is obvious, but do newspapers, such as the *New York Times*, have the culture to do what is necessary to adapt to the changing world?

It is common knowledge that newspapers have been struggling since the launch of the World Wide Web in 1993. That perspective is mostly—but not completely—right.

Some analyses about the decline of newspapers have put the onus on the value of the content, which, it is claimed, doesn't rival some distant Golden Age, such as the Watergate era when breaking a story in the *Washington Post* and other newspapers could bring down a president. But the fact is that the Internet has enabled newspaper content to reach a larger audience than ever before. Nielsen Online data shows that the top 25 U.S. news websites reached an average of 342 million unique monthly visitors in 2011.

The problem is monetizing that readership.

The economic downsides for newspapers since the advent of the Internet have been many. With its long-tail display advertising, the Internet also brought with it inexpensive ad inventory that has driven down cost per thousand (CPM) prices and made it difficult to generate online revenue for newspaper sites (as well as most other Internet sites).

What may have been even worse is the rise of brands that compete with newspapers' cash cow—the classified section. Companies like Monster.com snatched money from newspapers' help wanted sections. And then Craigslist, which offers online classified ads for free siphoned money away from the rest of the classified section.

Overall classified revenue in U.S. newspapers has not increased since the first quarter of 2006, according to the Newspaper Association of America (NAA). Similarly, overall newspaper advertising revenue in the United States has declined every quarter since the second quarter of 2006, also according to the NAA's data.

Newspapers do have a customer focus in general. They, however, have two distinct customer groups they serve: advertisers and readers. This duality makes it difficult to have a laser focus on any single segment of customers.

But newspapers' true downfall has been one of a shift in the culture of both of those audiences. As a rule, newspapers have not embraced data-driven cultures. Let's look at the *New York Times* as an example. If the *New York Times* had had a data-driven culture at its core, it might have acquired Monster.com and preserved its job listings stronghold.

The people who are attracted to the New York Times Company are more concerned with the *New York Times*, the newspaper, than the New York Times, the company. Even if the data indicated that acquiring Monster.com was a good business move, it wasn't really on the radar of most newspapers, whose culture focused on creating good journalism first and making money second. The culture regards Pulitzers and Polks more highly than it does shrewd revenue decisions.

The *New York Times*—despite building a top-notch website and embracing the metered access model, which has produced more than 700,000 paying digital subscribers—is, by its own account, still struggling with the digital world. An internal report, "Innovation," leaked in March 2014, fingered the *New York Times*' own culture as playing the key role in the company not taking full advantage of digital opportunities.

The report began, "The *New York Times* is winning journalism. . . . At the same time, we are falling behind in a second critical area: the art and science of getting our journalism to readers." The report said the *Times*' newsroom had not embraced a "digital-first" view of the world, and the front page of the print newspaper still ruled the minds of the editors. The newsroom, the report said, needs "to become a more nimble, digitally focused newsroom that can thrive in a landscape of constant change."

Still, while the *New York Times* may be perceived to be in financial trouble, it increased its revenue in the first quarter of 2014 and posted a small profit of $1.7 million on revenue of $390.4 million. The fact that the report exists is a sign that maybe the newspaper (and the company) can shift its culture and continue, despite competition from Buzzfeed, the Huffington Post, ProPublica, and Vox, to be profitable in the future.

Missed Opportunity

Even data-driven, customer-focused companies such as General Electric (GE) don't always take advantage of every opportunity, as this tale of a missed chance demonstrates.

General Electric has a reputation as a data-driven business with a customer focus, and deservedly so. But that doesn't mean it hasn't overlooked an opportunity every once in a while.

In 2010, GE said it wanted to create a solar power business that would rival its $6 billion wind energy business. But as prices plunged and American manufacturers were undercut by Chinese solar panel manufacturers, GE delayed the opening of a solar panel manufacturing plant two years later.

Despite data indicating that a form of Moore's law had taken hold in solar panels, with the cost of photovoltaic cells decreasing as their power increased, GE didn't make the investment in the business that it had planned. But while GE sat on the sidelines, a start-up called SolarCity developed a business model that is taking advantage of the sudden boom in solar panels, according to "As Solar Panels Boom, It Was the Simple Business Model That the Big Energy Players Missed," an insightful story written by Katie Fehrenbacher for GigaOm in 2014.

SolarCity finances and installs solar panels for residences and businesses. As such, it rides the sudden wave in interest in solar panels. In the first quarter of 2014, solar power accounted for 70 percent of the new energy that went on line, according to the Solar Energy Industry Association.

The growth stems from a combination of things: high energy costs in general and decreasing costs of solar power, in part because of the decline in the price of silicon.

In the spring of 2014, GE CEO Jeffrey Immelt acknowledged that GE had missed an opportunity. "My God, I wish I had thought of that," Fehrenbacher quoted Immelt saying in her story.

The thing is that Immelt was already familiar with the SolarCity model, because SunEdison had pioneered the approach in 2003. Immelt had spoken at an event with SunEdison founder Jigar Shah in 2007.

In a tweet subsequent to the GigaOm story, Shah said of Immelt, "He didn't miss SunEdison, he ignored it."

Whistling Past the Graveyard?

Comcast's pending acquisition of Time-Warner Cable indicates that the company has a clear understanding of the data that shows Netflix and other brands beginning to eat away at its market share. But can Comcast change its culture enough to become customer focused and maintain its dominance?

Is Comcast a customer-focused company? That would be hard to argue for Comcast or any other cable TV provider. It's hard to pass yourself off as customer focused when there was a feature film, *The Cable Guy*, inspired by your reputation for poor service. It doesn't help, either, that a Consumerist poll found that Comcast was voted "Worst Company in America."

If Comcast isn't customer focused, is it data driven? It may be. Comcast appears to know that the pay TV market may have reached its peak. The number of pay TV subscribers declined by 251,000 to about 100 million in 2013, according to SNL Kagan. That may be one reason why Comcast has agreed to merge with Time-Warner Cable in a deal valued at $45.2 billion, according to a press release issued by Comcast in February 2014. It wants to show growth one way or another and as quasimonopolies in many markets, cable companies have reason to want to combine—they can better control pricing.

The problem with Comcast and other pay TV operations is that their customers don't like them and are looking for any way to get their television elsewhere, especially if it's cheaper. Connected TVs may provide that opportunity. While just 27 percent of TVs shipped in 2011 were connected TVs, 80 percent of TVs shipped in 2015 will be connected TVs, according to Futuresource Consulting. Devices like Roku and services like Netflix provide a much more customer-friendly experience and may one day have traditional pay TV companies, such as Comcast, on the run.

Schadenfreude?

Start-ups in Silicon Valley are wading into financial technology, known as fintech. Can these new companies combine a data-driven and customer-focused approach to oust the current banking leaders?

As a Wall Street investment bank, Goldman Sachs is data driven and employs scores of quants. The question is whether Goldman Sachs is customer focused.

Goldman Sachs was data driven enough to realize in 2008 that collateral debt obligations—yes, the CDOs that helped cause the global financial crisis—were a bad investment. But if the bank is customer focused, that didn't stop it from selling those questionable CDOs to its customers.

From Goldman Sachs to local banks, which charge fees even for so-called free checking, Americans are largely dissatisfied with banks. Financial institutions seem much more like data-driven shareholder-focused businesses than data-driven customer-focused businesses.

The banking industry's lack of focus on the customer may give a start-up a chance to disrupt the banking industry. Silicon Valley is trying, according to a June 1, 2014, *New York* magazine article, "Is Silicon Valley the Future of Finance?" written by Kevin Roose. "Financial start-ups—known collectively as 'fintech'—are spreading like kudzu, each with a different idea about how to usurp the giants of Wall Street by offering better services, lower fees, or both," Roose wrote in the article.

He noted that these fintech start-ups raised $1.3 billion in the first quarter of 2014. Perhaps one day one or more of these start-ups will generate a data-driven innovation that will make consumers happy and Wall Street uncomfortable. If that day comes, it may provide some schadenfreude to taxpayers still angry at bailing out Goldman Sachs and the rest of Wall Street in the wake of the financial crisis.

CHAPTER 12

Using Data Responsibly

It's clear that corporations have a lot of data on their customers and prospects. In fact, there is no shortage of incidents where the question arises of whether corporations have crossed the line into knowing far too much about consumers:

- In one high-profile incident, a couple in suburban Chicago received a direct mailer from OfficeMax, which had an unusual element in the address stamped on it: "Daughter Killed in Car Crash" read one of the lines of the address.

  All of the information on the envelope was correct: the recipient's name, the street address, and the fact that the couple's 17-year-old daughter had been killed about a year earlier in a car accident. The couple was taken aback, shocked that a corporation seemed to know the family's sad history, let alone that it was maintained in a database, and more, inexplicably printed on a piece of junk mail.
- A story in the *New York Times Magazine*, "How Companies Learn Your Secrets" (February 16, 2012), showed how big box retailer Target was mining data to anticipate its customers' needs. Based on certain customer purchases, such as unscented lotion and calcium supplements, Target identified some customers as likely to be pregnant, according to the story. If a customer purchased particular items, Target would send her offers tailored to pregnant women.

  In one case described in the *Times*'s story, a puzzled father visited Target and asked the company to stop sending these offers to his daughter, who was still in high school. He accused Target of encouraging her to get pregnant, and a manager apologized. Shortly afterward, the manager followed up by calling the father to apologize again. Sheepishly, the man acknowledged that he had since discovered that his daughter was, indeed, pregnant.
- It is very common for consumers to visit a retailer's website—let's use online shoe retailer Zappos as an example—and then have ad after ad for that company appear as they browse

elsewhere on the Internet. It's a common form of what is known as retargeting.

Each of these examples—from the ads that seem to follow consumers around the Internet to the uncannily precise direct response offers from OfficeMax and Target—shows the power of big data to help companies use their marketing to reach consumers with accurate messages. Of course, these stories also serve as examples of why some consumers have significant privacy concerns.

In this age of big data, surveys consistently indicate that consumers have concerns about their privacy. A Pew Research Center study conducted in 2013 found that half of Internet users were concerned by the amount of public information about them available online, up from one-third in 2009. Pew also found that 86 percent of Internet users had taken some steps to cover their so-called digital footprints. And the study revealed that 55 percent of Internet users had "taken steps to avoid observation by specific people, organizations, or the government."

A survey conducted in 2013 by the Digital Advertising Alliance (DAA) asked Internet users what they most feared online. About 39 percent said identity theft was their top fear, followed by malware/viruses (34 percent) and government surveillance (12.3 percent). The DAA survey found that behaviorally targeted advertising was the top fear of only 4.4 percent of Internet users.

A survey by SDL plc, a content management and analytics company, showed that consumers are ambivalent about privacy and their relationships to corporations. On one hand, 65 percent of American consumers said they were worried about their personal information being used by marketers. At the same time, 80 percent of consumers said they were more likely to provide personal information to a trusted brand.

With the amount of digital data collected about them, consumers are right to have concerns about privacy protection. Ultimately, the use of big data by a business can create outsized returns and deliver phenomenal, relevant, and often free experiences for its customers. However, this comes with a responsibility for companies to use the information in a responsible and thoughtful way and requires commonsense approaches to building privacy and increased security considerations into an enterprise's big data practices.

In examining what should be done to firm up consumer privacy protection, we're going to address advertising and corporate databases separately, because although they are both powered by big data, they are quite different cases of consumer information.

Privacy and Online Advertising

First, let's look at the privacy concerns raised by online advertising and retargeting. The best companies are embracing complete transparency when it comes to consumers' privacy concerns and online advertising.

Zappos, the shoe retailer, is an example of how companies can be completely transparent about retargeted advertising. Some Internet users find the practice of retargeting disturbing ("creepy" seems to be most the commonly used adjective by detractors) and view it as an invasion of privacy. In its retargeting ads, Zappos addresses consumer concerns head-on with remarkable candor. The online shoe retailer recognizes that consumers have differing perspectives on retargeting, so it uses its advertising to help viewers understand what is happening and allows them to opt out of this kind of marketing.

Here's how Zappos does it. The company's retargeted ads include text that reads, "Why am I seeing this ad?" If consumers click on that text, they are taken to a page that explains retargeting and allows them to opt out. "Some people prefer rainbows. And other people prefer unicorns. If you prefer not to see personalized ads, we totally get it. OPT OUT HERE." The page goes on to reassure the consumer that none of his or her personal information has been shared with anyone. The process is entirely anonymous, and the ad was served solely based on the Zappos pages the consumer visited and an algorithm that determined which shoes the company could advertise that would most often lead to more sales.

The data that determines what ad you are served when you arrive at a particular website is often determined by the data contained in cookies that various websites and companies have placed on your web browser. These cookies give a digital picture of your browsing habits. Plus, if you have login information stored on particular sites, cookies can also provide information such as your name, address, and e-mail account. There are laws that place limits on how marketers can use this information. The more sensitive the information, the more heavily regulated its use becomes. For example, the use of financial data about a consumer is regulated by multiple laws such as the Fair Credit Reporting Act. The use of highly sensitive health data is regulated by the Health Insurance Portability and Accountability Act (HIPAA).

Despite these laws in place to regulate use of the underlying information stored in cookies about consumers, a battle about how businesses should use cookies continues. Some companies and organizations have advocated for the elimination of the third-party cookie—or at least they aim to marginalize the technology. Many privacy advocates have supported "do not track" (DNT), which is a tool that enables consumers to signal to websites that they do not want their actions and browsing habits to be tracked as they surf the web.

But arguments focused solely on cookies are a red herring. The issue isn't the cookie. The cookie is just a technology. There are other tracking technologies out there, such as statistical ID, a locally shared object (which is also known as a Flash cookie), the AdID reportedly being developed by Google, or a similar technology Microsoft is said to be creating. Cookies or any of these technologies are just tools. They can be used for good, safe, and effective advertising within the laws that currently exist on the books. Or those who don't care about laws can use them for bad purposes.

To get at the solution, we believe that the industry needs to focus on the actual problem it is trying to solve: that malevolent parties could take advantage of technologies such as cookies for their gain at the expense of our privacy as consumers. The solution could easily be accomplished through screening for enforcement of the rules to govern the use of information and through technical capabilities to block those that don't follow the rules.

As a result, only companies that pass this screening will have the privilege of targeting consumers, and for those that pass initial screening, any future misuse of this targeting information would have a penalty so severe—the inability to target most consumers online—that marketers won't be able to take the risk of noncompliance.

Ultimately, the core principles of good, effective ad targeting coexisting with consumer privacy must remain intact regardless of the cookie or other technologies being used to actually target the marketing messages. Any set of rules governing the Internet and how consumers interact with corporations—and vice versa—must acknowledge the following.

Tracking is a fact. Consumers will be tracked. Whether it's the cookie or some other technology, businesses will track consumers on the Internet. From a business standpoint, the capability to customize and personalize content and advertising is a key element separating the Internet from other media.

Transparency is essential. Businesses must be completely transparent about how they use tracking technology. Most reputable businesses post privacy policies on their websites, but few consumers read them. The best businesses should be more proactive and up front about informing consumers what information they're collecting from, for example, visitors to their website. American businesses would be well advised to follow their British counterparts, who use pop-up windows to inform new website visitors that the site is using cookies and visitors have the option to turn them off.

Users must have control. Users should have the ability to turn off the tools tracking them. There is a certain group of people who simply don't want to be tracked on the Internet and no amount of explaining how the tracking is anonymous and depersonalized will convince them otherwise. "The message should be: 'You guys are in control, and here are simple and easy ways to opt out,'" said Scott Meyer, Ghostery CEO. Marketers and publishers on the web should focus on the nearly 7 in 10 Internet users who never or rarely turn on the "do not track" setting in their browsers.

Content and advertising must be targeted, relevant, and convenient. Delivering content that is extremely targeted, relentlessly relevant, and instantaneously convenient is the essence of publishing on the Internet. For marketers and consumers alike to get the most value from the web, and to ensure that they continue to drive competition and underwrite Internet content, the advertising must also be targeted and relevant. Tracking is what enables that for both publishers and marketers.

Online data must be secured. Businesses need to have a more urgent recognition that the data they have access to can harm consumers in certain situations. The publishers, the marketers, and the companies that build the advertising exchanges that make programmatic advertising possible must make sure the data they use to target customers is non–personally identifiable information (non-PII) and protected and secure from the malevolent parties and hackers who would use that data for theft, blackmail, and other crimes.

Privacy and the Corporate Database

Corporate databases, in either analog or digital form, have existed as long as there has been commerce. Because of their longtime existence and the fact that they can contain sensitive personal information, ranging from Social Security numbers to medical diagnoses, these databases are overseen by significantly more government regulation than the relatively new (and continually innovating) technologies that run the online advertising ecosystem.

Laws regulating databases include HIPAA, the Fair Credit Reporting Act (FCRA), Gramm-Leach-Bliley Act (GLBA), Children's Online Privacy Protection Act (COPPA), and others. Corporate databases often contain sensitive information. The examples involving OfficeMax and Target at the beginning of this chapter certainly show that to be true. But let's take a closer look at these examples to determine how these incidents occurred—and whether anyone's privacy was truly breached.

Look at the case of the OfficeMax mailer that included the phrase "Daughter Killed in Car Crash." How did that phrase get imprinted on that mailer? A human being had to do it, right? Well, yes and no. As near as anyone can tell, that phrase was entered into a company database at a small Ohio retailer called Things Remembered Inc., according to a January 2014 *Wall Street Journal* story, "How a Family Tragedy Landed in a Retailer's Mailing." Why would someone at that company do that? The phrase was probably entered as a notation explaining the reason for a purchase; apparently, friends of the couple bought digital picture frames containing photos of the daughter from the retailer.

When Things Remembered offered its mailing list for sale, the phrase in question apparently came along with it, perhaps on an Excel spreadsheet. The phrase was automatically included and folded into other lists, which OfficeMax bought from a third party. Often these lists are scrubbed to ensure that there are no obscene words entered by bored data entry employees. Whatever scrubbing was done on this list missed the fateful words that were inadvertently included in the mailing list and on the envelope that wound up in the couple's mail.

"I can only speculate that one of these third-party companies tracked that death, and that got mis-keyed; it got merged in where it didn't belong," Edward Malthouse, a professor of integrated marketing communications at Northwestern University, told the *Chicago Tribune*. "I think it's a two-edged sword. On one hand as consumers, we want the advertising we see to be relevant, because advertising that's not relevant is spam. . . . There's a fine line between improved targeting and creepiness. This sounds like it was just a really boneheaded mistake."

OfficeMax, because it ultimately sent the mailer, found itself at the center of this controversy. But before the mailer became public, it is unlikely anyone at OfficeMax knew the family or that the family had a daughter who died. The information was locked away in a third-party database and likely no one at OfficeMax would have known this information was there, simply because there was no business reason to know it.

Certainly, OfficeMax did not want the phrase "Daughter Killed in Car Crash" on the mailer. It didn't want to offend a potential customer. It didn't want to create an embarrassing public relations disaster. And this is one thing about privacy: most corporations know there's a line, and they don't want to cross it.

It's the same situation for Target and its system for ascertaining that a customer may be pregnant. The company understands that its mailers offering baby clothes and cribs may alarm expectant mothers, who perhaps haven't yet told family and friends of their pregnancy. Target, according to the *New York Times Magazine* story on its data mining, also included deals on lawn mowers to mask the retailer's insight into the expectant mother's condition.

With the rise of the marketing stack (the marketing automation systems, the data management platforms, and the customer relationship management software), businesses have more insight into their customers than ever. But even with this information, these businesses want to comply with the law. And perhaps even more important in a highly competitive marketplace, they need to respect their relationship with their customers, as individuals and as a group.

In reality, they don't know their customers as individuals, even if their algorithms and marketing automation programs can offer that illusion and anticipate customers' needs and preferences automatically and at scale.

The Responsibility of Corporations

At the same time, it's certainly true that corporations have access to very personal and sensitive customer information, including Social Security numbers, credit card information, and purchase history. And while most businesses adhere to the laws in place to protect their customers' privacy, there are some who break laws regarding personal data. And that is where the real issue with the sensitive information contained in corporate databases lies. It's not in corporations crossing the bounds of privacy; it is in cybercriminals who want to raid these databases to extract the valuable data from them.

Certainly, corporations pay a public relations and financial price when their databases are compromised or sensitive information is breached. For instance, Sprint was recently taken to task when an employee allegedly shared via Facebook photos of a couple having sex. The employee had apparently uploaded the photos from a traded-in phone. Sharing its customer's private photos or data is not in Sprint's best interests. A story about the incident, "Lawsuit Says Sprint Worker Put Customer Sex Photos on Facebook," appeared in the *Los Angeles Times* and spread across the Internet. Sprint issued the following statement: "Protecting customer privacy is of the utmost importance to Sprint. We take these matters very seriously. We intend to fully investigate this matter."

Target was also involved in a serious financial and security breach when thieves stole millions of credit card numbers by hacking into the retailer's payment system. Ultimately, Target took a charge of $61 million for the incident.

Big data can create tremendous returns for businesses and at the same time a phenomenal experience for their customers: a true win-win. At the same time, businesses don't always invest in the appropriate safeguards to protect the sensitive customer data they have (credit card numbers, Social Security numbers, their birthdays, and more) if they don't have to. But this state of affairs has to change. For one thing, businesses must shift their perspective.

They need to develop a better understanding of the magnitude of the social contract they have entered into with customers when they fill their databases with sensitive and private consumer data. Businesses must have more respect for the data they have on customers and place more value on protecting that data. They must also have a better awareness of what the cybercriminals around the globe are capable of.

Todd Davis, chairman and CEO of Lifelock, a company that helps consumers protect their personal data, said the realization that more must be done to handle this problem is growing. He proposed three key steps to handling this problem of database security.

The first step to improving data security is consumer awareness. Davis's company, Lifelock, was built to educate consumers and protect them from the dangers of identity theft. Consumers need to understand their options when their personal data is breached, Davis said.

"Even if you're part of a data breach, we've got your back. You're not going to be out a bunch of time and money," Davis said.

With this message, Lifelock has grown for 35 consecutive quarters; it has more than 3 million customers, and generated $369.7 million in revenue in 2013. Davis believes that the more consumers are aware of database security issues, the more businesses will do to protect consumers.

Which brings us to the second step necessary to improve data security: enterprises must pay heightened attention to the protection of their customer databases. "There are best practices," Davis said, but he pointed out that many companies are simply not taking basic steps to protect their consumer data. In 2011, Verizon and the U.S. Secret Service Agency conducted a study and issued their Data Breach Investigation Report, which found that 89 percent of the companies that experienced a data breach in 2010 were not in compliance with the Payment Card Industry Data Security Standard.

Adrian Lane, an analyst with security consulting firm Securosis, outlined two basic ways that businesses can secure customer data.

First, they can secure the database that stores the data by patching and securely configuring the database, allowing only select employees access, and even placing the database behind a firewall. Second, they can protect the data and then they can encrypt data elements; or they can mask the data, by, for instance, replacing a real person's name with a pseudonym in the database; or they can "tokenize" the data by, for example, blocking out complete credit card or Social Security numbers and giving employees access to the last four digits only.

But Lifelock's Davis said even increased vigilance by enterprises won't be enough to completely protect consumer data. "If cyber-criminals want in bad enough, they can get in," Davis said.

The third step is giving legislation and law enforcement more teeth when it comes to cybercrime. Legislation must increase requirements for businesses regarding notification of data breaches and security requirements, and there must be stiffer penalties for companies that don't meet minimum standards of security.

Additionally, Davis said, the penalties must be increased for cybercrime. As it stands now, a bank robber who walks into a bank and steals $5,000, which is about the average take for such crimes, is highly likely to be caught and typically faces a mandatory sentence of five years. It's a much different situation for a cyber-criminal. "If you go to the same institution, commit identity theft, and withdraw money from my savings account, you have a less than 1 percent chance of getting caught, and there's not mandatory sentencing," Davis said. "First-time offenders have a good chance of getting parole. That's crazy. We don't have the right deterrents in place."

Ultimately it's all about the culture of an organization and the focus on treating data responsibly. LinkedIn is an example of a company that has "Member First" as a core tenet, and it literally lives and breathes this concept in everything it does. Every employee is required to get trained on its tenets, its privacy policies, and the data use policies. It also maintains a cross-functional Trust Council that meets monthly to help ensure that the company is living up to its promises. As LinkedIn says about its policies, "We always aim for clarity, consistency, and member control." By training all employees on these concepts and monitoring for compliance, they have taken a leadership position in treating data responsibly that other companies could emulate.

CHAPTER 13

Big Data's Big Future

The software, the tools, and the storage to make big data a component of your business are here. Now, the trick is to find the right people, the right resources, and the right opportunities to make the most of them in your company.

Most businesspeople agree that if the Era of Big Data isn't here yet, it's coming. And when used properly it can truly help a business succeed. According to "Big Data Insights and Opportunities," a report from IT industry association CompTia, more than three out of every four executives surveyed said that if they could harness big data, their companies would be stronger.

The rub is that almost the same percentage of executives queried in the same survey acknowledged that "Converting volumes of data into actionable intelligence has been a challenge."

We now have the technology, the marketing stack, and all the tools to analyze data. But making the best use of it, finding the signal in the noise, and discovering which pieces of data are most significant to your business—those are difficult tasks. They require a team made up of both creative and mathematically oriented individuals to determine what the data means and then to use that information to persuade others to buy your products or services.

Florian Zettelmeyer, professor of marketing at Northwestern University's Kellogg School of Management, said an often-overlooked part of building a big data machine is the people who will operate it. A dashboard means little if there's no one who can drive the car.

"There is a view out there that is heavily supported by the technology providers, who probably have the biggest stake in this market, that it is all a matter of having sort of the right dashboard and the right tools," Zettelmeyer said. "Then you don't really have to worry very much about the details. Everything is going to be just fine, and you know how to make decisions. I think that is, regrettably, really, really wrong."

Zettelmeyer says managers still have to know how to read the data, interpret it, and put their conclusions into action. "That is a big management skills upgrade that is required, not a technical skills upgrade," he said.

So how will the marketers of tomorrow (and by tomorrow, we don't mean only the distant future: we mean the literal day after today) make the best use of big data regarding their customers and prospects? It's always hard to predict even the near future, but one thing is clear: for the most successful companies, data and people will be at the center of it.

Jim Fowler, who founded Jigsaw and subsequently sold it to Salesforce.com in 2010 for $142 million, according to TechCrunch, said that technology is inevitably expanding the reach and scale of sales and marketing and how companies interact with their customers and prospects. Harnessing data is as much a necessity in this technology-dependent world as it once was to integrate the telephone in commerce, incorporate the automobile into a business model, and embrace e-mail marketing as part of your promotional strategy.

"Back three or four or five generations ago, our great-great-grandfathers might have visited their clients on a horse; our grandparents, in cars; and how many customers or prospects could someone touch in a given day given those parameters? Well, the answer was one, maybe two," Fowler said.

Now, with e-mail and other automated systems, sales and marketing can touch virtually anyone in their target audience in a matter of minutes. "With automated systems, which just get more and more complex, you have the ability to touch everyone," Fowler added. "So people who do a lot of buying are going to quit answering their e-mails and phones."

The difficulty of reaching prospects via traditional methods and the irresistible scale of reaching prospects via digital methods means that the next frontier is data. Sales and marketing professionals must make sure that when they do engage with a prospect, whether online or offline, the interaction is relevant and timely and useful. Using data intelligently to focus on customers and prospects will be key to growth for successful companies.

How Cleversafe Harnessed the Power of Data

For the myriad of companies that have not yet embraced data-driven marketing, a company like Cleversafe offers a hint of the future's possibilities. Cleversafe is an enterprise data storage company, one that has coders and engineers on staff who understand how to use technology and data to optimize business.

Cleversafe's target market includes film and television production companies that need to store massive amounts of data. Chris Gladwin, vice chairman and founder of Cleversafe, said his marketing team used basic data from the company's current customer list to identify approximately 6,000 new companies that could be its customers. These meet the number of employees, the revenue threshold, and storage needs that characterize Cleversafe's current customers.

Cleversafe then built a database of these 6,000 target companies. The database includes the names, e-mail addresses (when available), and any information they were able to collect about individual executives who are the storage decision makers at those companies. Cleversafe built this database by consulting its sales team, combing the Internet, buying industry mailing and e-mail lists, and even having summer interns cold-call the target companies to collect data on the decision makers, Gladwin said.

The company's original database included 15,000 targets. Gladwin estimates that the database currently contains about 30,000 names of people who influence storage purchase decisions at the target companies. Cleversafe uses Marketo marketing automation software and the Salesforce.com customer relationship management (CRM) system to track interactions with these individuals.

Using cookies, IP address identification via its Marketo software, and other techniques, Cleversafe is able to identify, accurately and consistently, when the people it is targeting visit the company website. When these prospects do visit, Cleversafe can deliver personalized content based on previous interactions. Cleversafe can also discern, for example, that a prospect company is researching a new storage purchase when a cluster of visits from several employees from that company occurs.

Cleversafe is relentlessly focused on communicating the right messages to the prospects it has identified. This focus is not reserved for online communications. When the company considers exhibiting at a trade show or sending salespeople to a conference, it sends its e-mail list to the event organizer and asks how many of the people on that list have committed to attend. If prospect attendance meets a minimum threshold, Cleversafe will commit to the event, often hosting a dinner for those prospects.

Key Trends Defining Big Data's Future

Cleversafe's database-focused marketing will be a characteristic of the best companies of the data-driven future. The best companies will focus relentlessly on determining their target market and target prospects and then spend money on marketing specifically to those targets. Using this simple but effective model, companies like Cleversafe can identify prospects, target those prospects, and then use nurturing tactics to drive them through the funnel. Personalization of messaging will be a key component of this style of marketing. Here are the trends central to big data's future.

Personalization

When some people hear the concept of personalization, they think immediately of sending e-mails or direct mail pieces that feature the prospect's name: "Dear Jimmy" or "Dear Suzy." That can be a part of personalization, but it is a small part and often one of dubious value. For instance, if a marketer uses a prospect's name too soon in the nurturing process, the prospect may find the overly personal tone creepy.

For most marketers, personalization is about serving the right content at the right time to the right person—and doing it at scale. To achieve that goal consistently, data and the technology to process it are necessities.

Marisa Edmund, vice president of marketing and communications at Edmund Optics, shared how her company is using software from Qubit to personalize and optimize EdmundOptics.com. "If I have a thousand customers coming to my website every day," Edmund said, "it's possible that each and every individual would see a different home page based on what they bought previously or what they liked or what they searched for on Google prior to coming to the site. If I have customers who always buy one product line, when they come back I'm going to show them that product line on the home page. Or if they search for prisms on Google, then they get to my home page, then they're going to see a lot more about prisms than they are about anything else."

In addition to just showing the right content, Edmund Optics can spur a prospect to make a deal by offering, for example, 10 percent off on the product the prospect appears to be searching for.

"The days of everybody having one home page that everybody sees are pretty much gone," Edmund said. Or at least they should be.

Tim Klausmeier, director of business intelligence at One Click Internet Ventures, takes a similar personalization approach at the Readers.com, SunglassWarehouse.com, and FelixandIris.com e-commerce websites he helps oversee. When One Click Internet Ventures launched these three sites, the focus was on search engine optimization and pay-per-click (PPC) techniques to drive raw traffic to the sites from prospects interested in buying eyewear. Recently, however, the company has shifted its focus to generating more repeat business from existing customers. This requires a personalization and a different user experience philosophy, Klausmeier said.

"Within the last year," he said, "we've turned our attention more to customer experience—not only pushing aggressively for new customer growth but really monitoring repeat business and starting to build the more sophisticated lifetime value models.

We're trying to understand what is getting customers to come back to our sites and what we can do within our business to really keep customers engaged with the brand."

A key to repeat business is personalizing the websites and making buying from Readers.com or SunglassWarehouse.com as frictionless as possible. On Readers.com, personalizing the experience can be as simple as focusing on the magnifying power of the reading glasses the visitor has purchased before. "You want to know what's in stock for your power and you want the whole site to revolve around that," Klausmeier said, adding, "Just continually giving that customer a more personalized experience, this is the next thing that we're really trying to zero in on."

Additionally, in creating a recommendation engine for customers, One Click Internet Ventures is borrowing from the king of e-commerce, Amazon.com. "We've teamed with a company called Certona on product recommendations," Klausmeier said. "We're sending recommendations based on click patterns in e-mails as well as on the site. You're seeing it with Amazon—customers are expecting a personalized experience and look for a site to put products in front of them that meet their needs. If a potential customer does not see what they want on your site right away, they are moving on to your competitor."

How You Can Get Started on Personalization The first step is to install some analytics software on your website. Google Analytics has a free version. Adobe Analytics (formerly Omniture SiteCatalyst) is another among many good options. Without an analytics tool to show you what's happening, you're in the dark about how to improve your website experience. It's like driving 100 miles per hour without headlights in the middle of the night. It won't end well.

Integrating Data Silos and Platforms

Marketers have data on prospects who have viewed their display ads, searched for their products on Google, opened their e-mails (or not), interacted with customer service, and purchased products via e-commerce. For most companies, however, the problem is that these databases remain separate and don't offer a 360-degree view of the customer. This disconnect hamstrings a marketer's capability to deliver the right message at the right time.

"It's combining the systems together in one place to give you the complete view of the customer," Heather Zynczak, CMO of Domo, said. "That's where the nirvana is."

Technologically, APIs and other tools are available to integrate these various systems. The main stumbling block for many companies is building the team and the processes capable of taking full advantage of the integration. Zynczak argues that the benefits are worth the effort, because incomplete data can lead to erroneous conclusions.

"You need data out of multiple places," Zynczak said. "Otherwise, you don't get the complete picture, and you have to have a complete picture. Otherwise, you make decisions with limited information, and you make the wrong decisions. I think this is why we've been so successful. Not only do we use Google Analytics, we use SiteCat as well, Adobe's SiteCatalyst, so we understand the conversion rates; we understand the click-through rates. We understand the traffic that comes in. We understand which landing pages work. We understand the targets. We know all those things which are pretty normal, but we also incorporate budget information, so that we know how much we're spending and what our goals were on spending."

As mobile continues its expansion, marketers must also integrate their data on customers and prospects on the desktop, on tablets, and on smartphones. "It's the same user whether they are on a desktop device, whether they are in social, whether they are looking at online video, whether they are running on a mobile smartphone or a tablet," said Mark Zagorski, CEO of eXelate, "and the smart marketer wants to be able to carry on a conversation with the same consumer across all of those channels, knowing what the sequence of messages has been prior and being able to be consistent about the messaging as opposed to random offers in random places with random frequencies."

One Click Internet Ventures' Klausmeier has attempted to integrate much of its customer data, and the company has used Domo dashboards to help facilitate this integration. One Click Internet Ventures has created a centralized database that unifies the company's PPC data, AdWords and Bing data, e-mail campaign data, and other interactions. At a very basic level, this system has simplified retrieving all the necessary data from a variety of databases. "It's so much easier to build out our monthly reports and track our metrics in real time with Domo. We no longer have to log in to multiple third parties to review our metrics; everything is just a click away," Klausmeier said.

The centralized database and dashboard have also made it easier for One Click Internet Ventures to monitor its goal of increasing repeat customer transactions and revenue. "We built out an internal lifetime value model, allowing us to see repeat revenue from a customer each month after their initial purchase. We monitor what marketing channels and campaigns our repeat revenue comes from and use this information to improve our retention efforts," Klausmeier said.

How You Can Get Started with Integrating Your Information Silos Integrate your data across various software systems. Marketers should begin the integration process by linking together their marketing automation software and their customer relationship management system. It offers the opportunity to track leads as they turn into revenue. As a bonus, it is also an opportunity to make sales and marketing work more closely together.

Marketing Measurement

Marketers can measure the impact of their programs better than was ever before possible. In the upper funnel, they can measure TV and display advertising's capability to drive more of their target audience to their corporate website. In the midfunnel, they can measure the impact of their nurturing programs and their ability to influence, engage, and educate prospects. And in the lower funnel, marketers can analyze the effects of search and e-mail and their ability to generate conversions, marketing qualified leads, and even revenue.

With the advanced attribution models that Adometry, Convertro, and VisualIQ have built, marketers can apply statistical models that allocate budgets efficiently across the entire funnel to make marketing spending more effective than ever before.

Vigilance about data allows marketers to use metrics to spend more on what's working and spend less on what's not. By embracing data, more marketers will be able to deftly maneuver their marketing, as Domo's Zynczak did with one program in particular:

"We ran a Google Ads display campaign where we thought it was amazing because we were getting really inexpensive top-of-the-funnel leads, and the conversion rate was through the roof," Zynczak said. "Then we found two weeks later that our cost per opportunity—which typically has a high close rate—was massively going through the roof. It was because the top-of-the-funnel leads we were getting off Google Ads display, even though they were achieving conversions, were actually terrible quality. So within two weeks, I shut that campaign off. I rejiggered and put the funds elsewhere."

How You Can Get Started with Marketing Measurement If you're not already measuring lower-funnel activities such as paid search and e-mail, start there. Measure how much traffic paid search is delivering to your website, how often those visitors convert by providing their e-mail addresses or buying, and how likely they are to become customers. Compare different tactics to each other to see what leads to the highest return on spend. Also rigorously measure your e-mail for open rates and responses, and strive for constant A/B testing and improvement.

Predictive Analytics

It's one thing to use data to analyze past behaviors. It's quite another to use data to predict future ones. More difficult still is using data to predict these future behaviors accurately.

A 2014 IBM study, "Stepping Up to the Challenge: CMO Insights from the Global C-Suite Study," found that 94 percent of CMOs said they intended to use advanced predictive analytics in the next three to five years—the exact same percentage of CMOs that the same study found planned to boost their mobile capabilities.

Predictive lead scoring companies are thriving. The businesses of Lattice Engines, Mintigo, and Infer are all booming. Nick Panayi, director of global brand and digital marketing at Computer Sciences Corporation, said that dashboards are valuable, but the real value lies in anticipating, sooner and more accurately than your competitors, what your customers want and giving it to them. "When it comes to the executive level as well as marketing team at large, we want everyone to have a dashboard where all those things come together in the form of KPIs and how you do against those KPIs," Panayi said. "It's very important to put it altogether. We use the technology called Good Data to do that, and where we're going to separate the good marketers from the great marketers will be determined by their ability to conduct predictive modeling. It's important to have dashboards, but dashboards are table stakes. They are what I call rearview mirror. What you do with that information in terms of predicting what comes next and helping your sales organization with that is what's going to be the keys to the kingdom going forward."

How You Can Get Started with Predictive Analytics While predictive analytics sounds expensive, like something reserved for the IBMs and Oracles of the world, the tools are not as expensive as you might think. They can deliver powerful insights about your customer base that can help you target prospects much more efficiently. Look at a company like FlipTop, which offers a 30-day free trial as of this printing. Other vendors include 6Sense, Mintigo, Lattice Engines, and Infer.

Mobile

In three years' time, Facebook moved from generating virtually zero percent of its revenue to 59 percent of its revenue from mobile devices. Smartphones throw off massive amounts of data, from geolocation to data and app usage to web surfing habits. LinkedIn predicts that it will have its "mobile moment," where greater than 50 percent of its global traffic will come from mobile, later in 2014. Mary Meeker at Kleiner Perkins Caufield & Byers, a highly successful Silicon Valley venture capital firm, recently noted in her "Internet Trends 2014" report that mobile now represents 25 percent of the global web usage.

So the world is now officially mobile. The challenge for marketers is to find the right messaging to reach users on smartphones with the small (but increasing) size of their screens, which provide a small canvas through which to reach consumers. Users say they don't want ads on their smartphones and find them annoying and disruptive, but they have said the same thing for marketing messages on radio, television, interstate highways, and the desktop Internet. Data-driven ads will come to mobile phones in great numbers; that's a certainty. The big long-term questions are what form will these marketing messages take, what technology will advertisers use to identify users, and how will this ID technology relate to the cookie and other digital identifiers?

Marketers are already finding that they must cater to mobile users even in the presence of still unwieldy methods for identifying users. Facebook, for instance, has taken a mobile-first design approach, said its CMO, Gary Briggs. All of the company's redesigns of its interface, for instance, must account for mobile as well as desktop. At the very least, other marketers have implemented responsive design so their websites automatically optimize for tablet and smartphone devices.

At One Click Internet Ventures, Tim Klausmeier says that his company is increasingly adapting its business model to mobile. "With reports we've been able to build out with Domo, we've seen how mobile and tablets have taken off on our sites," he said. "Domo has also allowed us to chart mobile conversion rates and revenue growth, which has helped us make decisions on where to allocate development resources on our sites."

How You Can Get Started with Mobile Pick up your smartphone, and key in your website. Can you read it and navigate it easily on your device? If so, you're ahead of the game. If not, get your designers to create a mobile site. Every day your mobile site is nonnavigable, you're losing business. Now, open one of your marketing e-mails on your phone. Can you easily read and react to that e-mail? Is it easy for a prospect to complete a transaction? If so, great! If not, optimize your e-mails for mobile just as you do your websites.

Internet of Things

Advanced marketers are adapting to mobile. Some slower-moving marketers are still getting their desktop websites up to speed. They need to act fast, because a new, more expansive version of the Internet is coming soon. It's called the Internet of Things, and it will generate more data than the desktop Internet and mobile Internet combined.

The Internet of Things refers to Internet-enabled machines that generate their own data. Common examples are jet engines that inform mechanics about maintenance or performance issues, tractors that share data on fuel consumption and geolocation, and refrigerators that remind users when they're out of butter or milk. There will be more connected TVs, smart homes, smart cars, and smart factories. The Internet of Things represents a powerful opportunity for marketers to learn more about customers and how they're interacting with their products.

Cisco Systems estimates that 50 billion machines will be online by 2020, up from 13 billion in 2013. In a recent LinkedIn post, "Why Our Machines' Inner Lives Are the Key to the Next Economic Revolution," General Electric CMO Beth Comstock said that this development is extraordinary. "For the first time in history, intelligence is spreading not only from person to person—it's spreading from human to machine, from machine to machine, and then back to humans," she wrote. "This communication, through the Industrial Internet, is going to create enormous value and improve outcomes for industries from health care to aviation to power and beyond."

The examples of how data from the Internet of Things is already being used run from the deadly serious to the comical. In Brazil, Kimberly-Clark has introduced Huggies with a sensor that alerts Mom and Dad—via a tweet—when their child has wet the diaper. The product is called TweetPee.

An InfoCommerce Group column lauded the position that Spiceworks has already staked out in the Internet of Things: "This company offers software that helps companies manage their computer networks—and everything connected to them. Spiceworks not only knows the make and model of every printer owned by hundreds of thousands of companies, it knows when they're running low on toner, and all in real time. Think of how many different ways you could monetize data like this!"

A McKinsey & Company report, "The Seven Habits of Highly Effective Digital Enterprises," noted that U.S. Xpress, a transportation company, collects data from its fleet via in-vehicle sensors. The company found that it could save $20 million in annual fuel consumption by eliminating engine idling in its vehicles.

Wearables produced by companies like Fitbit, which track a user's exercise and eating habits, also generate huge amounts of data. Google, which has a wearable of its own in Google Glass, is investing heavily in the Internet of Things. It acquired Nest, which manufactures a smart thermostat, for $3.2 billion. Apple is also said to have an eye on developing a system for smart houses. There are early prototypes of potentially lifesaving sensor pills that, when swallowed, harmlessly attach to the stomach lining and can detect concentrations of medication in the body and e-mail doctors when a patient is missing a dose.

In addition to throwing off all of this data, the Internet of Things also provides a monetization opportunity via advertising. In a 2014 letter to the Securities and Exchange Commission, Google wrote, "We expect the definition of 'mobile' to continue to evolve as more and more 'smart' devices gain traction in the market. For example, a few years from now, we and other companies could be serving ads and other content on refrigerators, car dashboards, thermostats, glasses, and watches, to name just a few possibilities."

How You Can Get Started with the Internet of Things Ask yourself what you'd like to know about how your customers use your product, and can your engineers design a sensor that will allow you to answer that question. This expansion of the Internet provides opportunities, especially for manufacturers.

Privacy and Security

Along with its possibilities, the Internet of Things adds another layer of complexity for digital security and privacy. A 2014 Spiceworks report, "The Devices Are Coming," which surveyed more than 400 information technology (IT) executives, found that 45 percent of these executives identified security as a top challenge in storing data generated by devices.

Even though laws are already on the books that protect Internet users' privacy online and in digital databases controlled by both corporations and government, it appears likely that at some point in the future the United States Congress will pass additional legislation that addresses consumer privacy and information protection.

Ideally, this legislation will outline the responsibility of product developers to give consumers the capability to control and opt out of being tracked on the Internet without restricting the ability of marketing technology companies to develop new products that have the promise to reduce the number of wasteful and poorly targeted advertisements the consumers receive.

In addition to legislation that raises penalties for database breaches that expose consumer credit cards and other private information, corporations must take their responsibilities more seriously for staying one step ahead of the cyber criminals and protecting the sensitive and valuable information they have on their customers.

How You Can Get Started with Privacy and Security The first step is making sure your customer database is as secure as it can be. Meet with your marketing and information technology teams to ensure that data security is a priority. Form a cross-functional "trust council," such as the one at LinkedIn, to focus on and highlight areas that might be problematic. You don't want to make a phone call to your best customers saying that sensitive payment information has been compromised. The second step is putting yourself in your customers' and prospects' shoes. Do you offer your clients transparency and control over the information being gathered? If not, you should think about how to implement this to provide more of both.

Product Development

The ways in which we use the window that data provides on customer behavior must be more than reactive. In the best cases it will be predictive. Analysis of customers' behavior—as they engage with software-as-a-service products or interact with products connected to the Internet—can also deliver insights that change the products offered by a company, or even change the company itself. Companies that are open to data and what it tells them must also be open to change to anticipate the changing needs of their customers.

Mark Zagorski from eXelate noted that product development is an area where companies can be big winners—if they listen carefully to the data.

"One of the things that always gets left out here is product, which I think you're going to see a much more aggressive movement and product differentiation and product development that will be influenced by big data," Zagorski said. "What most people talk about when it comes to data is marketing and messaging, social media, and all these kind of things, but what you really start thinking is: how is this going to affect product development? Product development is going to move toward a much more real-time switch, in which we are not just positioning our product, but in a way we can actually create products based on the information that we're seeing in real time."

How You Can Get Started with Product Development First, get in front of your customers and immerse yourself in how they're using your products and services. Don't just rely on focus groups. Literally sit and watch them use your product. We guarantee you'll learn something. Then, sit down with the people who know your customers the best, whether it's sales, marketing, finance, or some other department. Make sure they know your company prizes innovation and that data on how customers are interacting (or not interacting) with your products may generate new product ideas that could be big winners. Form an e-mail alias that the company can use to provide feedback that is read consistently by executives and product managers and assign a specific person to own the responses and collection of that data.

Social Media

Social media promises to deliver rich data for marketers. For advertisers, it offers targeting opportunities, as target audiences on LinkedIn, Facebook, and Twitter have identified themselves and their interests in their profiles and in how they interact with their networks.

Social media also offers incredible amounts of both unstructured and structured data. With this data, marketers can, if they commit to doing so, respond to positive or negative comments in real time. They can address customer service issues, also in real time. And they can take special care of big-time social media influencers who have mentioned their brand, either positively or negatively.

Technology is appearing for both marketers and salespeople to mine the data available on social media networks and use it to their advantage. Sprinklr is software that is designed to create an infrastructure for enterprise companies to implement to take advantage of social media. With Sprinklr, marketers can build processes and tools for marketers to respond to tweets and posts in real time to head off customer complaints and amplify customer praise.

Nimble is another company that has built technology to help companies exploit the constant data flow of social media. In Nimble's case, the company has created its software to help small sales teams gain insight into their customers and prospects in real time.

Jon Ferrara, CEO of Nimble, says that they built Nimble to provide business professionals with the intelligence they need to connect with their clients in a more authentic and relevant way. Nimble is designed to review information from dozens of sources around the web, including Twitter, LinkedIn, Facebook, Google+, Instagram, and Foursquare, and collects public information into a resource that helps salespeople to be better prepared for sales calls, meetings, and interviews.

"Nimble," Ferrara said, "automatically logs e-mail conversations and social connections, making it easy for you to set a stay-in-touch cycle. Follow-up is key to nurturing and maintaining great business relationships; that's why we give you Nimble to do all this for you and remind you when it is time to reconnect."

Nimble has built a technology that integrates with e-mail to provide a broader picture of how a specific customer or prospect is behaving online. "Imagine if you had an app inside your inbox that provided a complete dossier and history of the person you're communicating with," Ferrara said. "We built our Smart Contacts App to empower business professionals to use Nimble's intelligent insights everywhere and anywhere they work."

What Nimble does for salespeople is track their prospects and customers wherever they appear online, including social media. These kinds of insights into what their targets are doing and saying online can be valuable for salespeople. "What we do is we bring in all of your most important signals—your e-mail, your calendar, your connections, your conversations, and all of your social signals—and then we layer intelligence on top of that," Ferrara said. "We look at the fingerprint of people you've successfully done business with before and identify new people for you to connect with and engage with."

How You Can Get Started with Social Media Many marketers start with producing content, and posting on Facebook, LinkedIn, and Twitter is probably a necessity. But listening on social media is a necessity, too, and using a listening software can be a good window for gaining insight on your industry, your customers, and your prospects. LinkedIn believes this is so important that it recently launched Sales Navigator, a product specifically built to help expose social triggers about sales opportunities.

Content Marketing

Content marketing might seem far from being a data-driven tactic, but it isn't. The most effective content marketing—whether it's blog posts, online videos, social media posts, or tweets—prompts your prospects to interact with your brand, long before they are willing to identify themselves. It also generates data that exposes where they are in the buying cycle.

In many industries prospects may interact with a brand or visit its website a couple dozen times—or even more—before they share their e-mail addresses. Up until that time, the content is painting a picture of your brand. It shows whether you're helpful, whether you're entertaining, and whether you're smart. All the while, the most effective content marketers are tracking with cookies or other technologies the anonymous prospects who read or watch or share the content. This tracking provides data on what content is working and, most important, what content leads to sales.

Content marketing is critical to data-driven marketers. It's why Bill Macaitis, former CMO of Zendesk, said that hiring a content team was his first step in building his data-driven marketing squad when he joined the company.

How You Can Get Started with Content Marketing The key is to hire people who can produce lots of clear, helpful, and entertaining content regularly. That doesn't necessarily mean hiring people with marketing experience. Sometimes the reporters and editors who cover your industry are the best bet. And because of the inexorable march of data and technology discussed in this book, many of them are looking for work.

Your Industry Will Not Escape

Big data has already transformed numerous industries—retail, entertainment, media, telecommunications, and the stock exchanges, to name a few. Big data has even impacted what is often termed the oldest industry, agriculture, as farmers now use data to predict the weather, optimize irrigation, and sell their yield at the highest possible price.

Big data is also poised to impact jet engine maintenance, said Geoffrey Moore, author of *Inside the Tornado*. "General Electric is very interested in predictive maintenance for aircraft engines," Moore said. "Rather than selling you an engine, General Electric would like to sell you flight miles, and then it will take care of everything. But in that kind of world, if you are going to make that promise, you have to have a huge big data back end that is continuously streaming information from the aircraft engines and maintenance depots."

Moore says, however, that the industries where big data may have the largest impact in the near future are education, government, and health care. "All three of them lend themselves to the capabilities of big data," he said. "All three have regulatory issues and privacy issues, but all three are in massive need of productivity improvement."

The most effective uses of big data thrive on transparency. Moore makes the case that the current educational system is far too opaque. "We really don't know what happens once the teacher goes into the classroom," he said.

The educational process, however, becomes more transparent once lessons take place on a computer. "If you put the educational lessons on an iPad, a lot of good things start to happen," Moore said. "One of them is you can see how the students are progressing through any body of material by simply looking at how many tests they've passed. From a big data point of view, you can see how the students are performing."

When the data indicates one approach is working better than another, education is using what amounts to A/B testing to boost the performance of both students and teachers. "You can automatically improve the quality of education simply by allowing students to vote up and vote down and teachers to vote up and vote down on various modules, interventions, and tests," Moore said. "All of a sudden, what was entirely opaque is now very transparent."

In the governmental arena, the National Security Agency's surveillance has clearly shown that a government agency can implement a large-scale program based on big data. Whether that program violates the Constitution is another matter, but government has also begun to use big data in less controversial ways.

"We are just seeing the early days of municipalities and government using big data," Moore said. "For example, we just eliminated the toll takers on the Golden Gate Bridge with automated tolling. And what if we had smart highways that would know where the traffic stops and how to reroute around it? Los Angeles is starting to use big data algorithms essentially to manage traffic at scale as opposed to locally optimizing it for a few traffic lights."

Health care may provide the most promising opportunity for big data's transformative powers. Deerwalk is one of many technology companies looking to use big data to remake the health care industry. Deerwalk has built a data platform that incorporates myriad data on patients for physicians and nurses to get immediate access to a patient's history. Patients also have access to the data on a web portal and can update information, such as their weight and fitness level, and report that back to their doctor. "The patient is seeing the same thing that the nurse is seeing," said Bill Higgins, Deerwalk's COO. "It's all shared data."

Deerwalk's platform incorporates data beyond what is available from claims data. "What has not been available to providers is the next level of information, biometric data: your height, your weight, your blood pressure, your LDLs [low-density lipoproteins], HDLs, triglycerides," Higgins said. "The data has your actual values from the test rather than just 'I had a blood test.'"

The ultimate goal is to deliver better outcomes to patients and lower costs to insurers. "Health care is being transformed because big data is allowing us to analyze this aggregated information that we've never been able to pull together before," Higgins said.

Blue Health Intelligence is a health care technology company that resembles Deerwalk in its use of big data. Blue Health Intelligence collects and mines the medical and pharmacy claims data for multiple Blue Cross Blue Shield Plans. This is the largest healthcare claims database in the country with more than 140 million individuals nationwide, collected over nine years. And, Blue Health Intelligence has the ability to link these records with clinical and lifestyle data.

"The whole purpose is to collect health care data on a national level and then use it to inform better decision making," said Swati Abbott, CEO of Blue Health Intelligence. "It works in two kinds of beneficial ways. One is reducing costs for the industry. The other is preventing a particular patient from getting worse or from getting sick in the first place if the data shows that they're more susceptible to a certain disease."

Consumers are making more healthcare decisions and purchases and need transparency. "This is where data and analytics can help to take complex healthcare data and make it simple for consumers," Abbott said.

How You Can Get Started Transforming Your Own Industry Like Health Care, Government, and Education Are Being Transformed Big data is coming to your sector of the business world. Do an inventory of the data flowing into your company. The most effective place to start could be analyzing your best customers, identifying what they have in common, and then targeting lookalikes as prospects.

The Human Touch Remains Essential

Behind first appearances and gut feelings, there is always data—data that sometimes showed a truth that was different than what it appeared to be. It took people analyzing and interpreting the data to see beyond the perception to the truth. Eratosthenes used data to prove the earth was round and determined its circumference. Copernicus used data to prove that the earth revolves around the sun when that was an opinion that could get you killed. And Nate Silver used data to find the signal in the noise to predict that Barack Obama would win the presidency in 2008 and 2012.

No matter how much you can measure, it takes people to determine the best use of data and to find the truth. We have software; we have massive data storage systems; we have handy analytics tools. All of these help us get at that truth that the data we have is showing us.

But it is vital that we have the right people looking at the data in the right way and drawing the correct conclusions. The term may be *big data*, but in the end it's the little triggers—little triggers identified by human beings—that will help businesses make the most of the information that's out there. A company can make the move to being a big data–driven business by having a laser focus on only the metrics that mean the most to its performance. The data is there, but it takes people to see it, to organize it, to interpret it, and to put their conclusions into action.

Big data may be a scary concept. But with the right people, right systems, and right cultures, it's something that businesses can get a handle on—especially when they concentrate on the data that is most important to their business and to their customers.

There's a big ocean of data waiting for you. If you want to win, jump in!

Index